D0667667

THE PROMISE
OF THEORY

THE JOHN DEWEY LECTURE—NUMBER NINETEEN

The John Dewey Lecture is delivered annually under the sponsorship of the John Dewey Society. This book is an elaboration of the Lecture given in 1982. The intention of the series is to provide a setting where able thinkers from various sectors of our intellectual life can direct their most searching thought to problems that involve the relation of education to culture. Arrangements for the presentation and publication of the Lecture are under the direction of the John Dewey Society Commission on Lectures.

D. Bob Gowin, *Chairperson and Editor*
Cornell University

THE PROMISE OF THEORY

EDUCATION AND THE POLITICS OF CULTURAL CHANGE

C.A. Bowers
UNIVERSITY OF OREGON

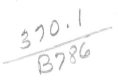

Longman
New York & London

The Promise of Theory

Education and the Politics of Cultural Change

Longman Inc., 1560 Broadway, New York, N.Y. 10036
Associated companies, branches, and representatives
throughout the world.

Developmental Editor: Lane Akers
Editorial and Design Supervisor: Thomas Bacher
Production Supervisor: Ferne Y. Kawahara
Manufacturing Supervisor: Marion Hess

Library of Congress Cataloging in Publication Data

Bowers, C. A.
    The promise of theory.
    (John Dewey lecture)
    Includes index.
    1. Educational sociology. 2. Educational equalization.
3. Education—Philosophy. I. Title. II. Series.
LC191.B675   1984   370'.1   83-805
ISBN 0-582-28419-8

Manufactured in the United States of America
Printing: 9 8 7 6 5 4 3 2 1   Year: 91 90 89 88 87 86 85 84

Contents

Preface

I had two main purposes in writing this book. The first was to call attention to the educational implications of the relativizing of traditional forms
of cultural authority that appears as an essential characteristic of modernization, with its emphasis on individualism, equality, and critical inquiry.
The second purpose was to show how the sociology of knowledge can be
used to develop a theory of education that addresses the challenge of
living in an era characterized by fundamental changes in how authority
is established and maintained. By juxtaposing a theory of education
against the background panorama of modernization, I am particularly
sensitive to the dangers of misinterpretations caused by a lack of
symmetry between the intention of the writer and the conceptual orientation of the reader. Modernization is an exceedingly complex phenomenon that has attracted the attention of seminal thinkers in the social
sciences (Karl Marx, Max Weber, and Emile Durkheim, to cite the most
notable examples), and it would be foolish to discuss modernization
without considering their contributions. I am not presuming that the
feature of modernization I have chosen to deal with is the most essential
or that the discussion opens up new territory. In many ways, Weber's
analysis of the connection between rationalization and modernization
appears to touch on the most basic characteristics of modern life. But
modern culture is characterized by a mix of increasingly diverse beliefs,
values, and social practices, with the result that contradictory tendencies
are commonplace. For example, the remissive mode of individualism, as
the Australian sociologist, John Carroll, has pointed out, has fostered a
permissive climate that paradoxically has led to a shift of authority from
individuals to institutions. A further example of the syncretism of modern
culture was called to our attention by Daniel Bell who noted the disjunction of value orientations that occur in the realms of techno-economic
activity, polity, and expressive culture. By putting in focus the relativizing
aspect of modern culture, I am not suggesting that the purposive ration-

alism Weber identified has disappeared, leaving us only with an empty ideology that no longer corresponds to the pattern that regulates our more substantive social activities. Nor am I suggesting that the relativizing tendencies within modern culture that are altering the basis of authority will erode the foundations of purposive rational behavior.

The argument is less grandiose and I hope more germane to the struggle against the seemingly unrelenting encroachment of institutions into the lives of individuals who are sensitive to the shaping and nourishing influence of cultural traditions on personal dignity and self-identity. The relativizing of traditional forms of cultural authority may be viewed, from a different perspective, as a transitional phase in how a cultural world view and social practice are to be organized. This transitional phase, which occurs in different areas of cultural belief and practice in the most irregular patterns, is characterized by a breakdown in the hold that traditional forms of cultural authority exerts on the members of society. As traditional forms of authority are delegitimatized individuals enter a brief period of liminal cultural space that allows for the negotiation of new meanings. The relativizing of traditional forms of authority provides, in effect, a moment in social time when the voice of the individual matters, and when there is the potential for new forms of authority to be established through a more democratic and educative process. The recent successes of the feminist movement provide an example of the liminal cultural space that results from challenging the authority of traditional social practices, linguistic conventions, and deep patterns of belief. As the hold of these traditional forms of cultural authority on the individual's natural attitude was broken, the opportunity emerged to renegotiate the definitions that would regulate new social relationships and ways of thinking. The relativizing of traditional authority that makes possible the negotiation of new meanings gives language a different form of political significance. The liminal cultural space created by the feminist movement fostered a more reflexive form of communication and growth in communicative competence. Discourse did not simply maintain the old cultural patterns, but became a political force in establishing new foundations.

The response to the liminal cultural space that arises when traditional practices and beliefs are delegitimatized is not always determined by the communicative competence of a significant segment of citizens. A more frequent occurrence is the exploitation of those opportunities by populist extremist groups, as well as by economic and governmental elites, who possess the power to impose their definitions in ways in which the new forms of authority serve their special interests. In many instances, people simply lack the knowledge necessary for the exercise of communicative competence, and thus the political power to define "what is" passes by default to those special interest groups that are able to impose their definitions. The current rationalizing of the teacher's work situation by administrators steeped in an ideology that has its roots in Taylorism is an example that shows that the liminality of disrupted traditions is not being resolved through a negotiation process involving participants equally adept in the exercise communicative competence. The continual on-slaught of technological innovation in both consumer and work sectors represents further examples of fundamental issues being settled in a one-sided manner rather than through the negotiation of meanings involving participants who represent diverse points of view. The ability to exercise communicative competence, and thus to participate in the political process that establishes the new basis of understanding and social prac-tice, has important implications for how we think about education. Consequently the development of a theory of education that leads to the fostering of the student's ability to participate in the negotiation process is one of the primary aims of this book.

Laying the groundwork for, such a theory has involved exploring the explanatory power of the sociology of knowledge. The ideas of Alfred Schutz, Peter Berger, and Thomas Luckmann, augmented by ideas borrowed from cultural anthropology and social linguistics, can be used to develop an approach to education that fosters communicative compe-tence. The sociology of knowledge is especially powerful in distinguishing the "moves" in the language game of socialization that empower the individual, from the "moves" that limit thought to the world of taken for granted belief. This theoretical framework is also useful for clarifying the contribution that curriculum changes can make to increasing the student's communicative competence. Although the basic writings of Schutz, Berger, and Luckmann are familiar to a significant number of educational theorists, few serious attempts have been made to think about the educational process from within the theoretical framework they have given us. The rapid change in intellectual orientations that characterized the middle 1960s and the early 1970s relativized the significance of their work, with the result that educational theorists were expected to be familiar with the essentials of their special vocabulary and theory but not to become too involved lest they risk the dangers of not keeping intel-lectually current. Since we seem to be entering a period of intellectual recession, where the search for new paradigms has undergone a marked decline, it is worthwhile to return to the sociology of knowledge frame-work for the purpose of exploring, at a more leisurely pace, its contri-bution in translating a democratically inspired theory of education into classroom practice.

For providing this opportunity I want to thank the John Dewey Society, and in particular Mary Anne Raywid, D. Bob Gowin, and members of the lecture commission. It took a degree of courage to invite a reexamination of a theory consigned to the dustbin of spent academic attractions. Their sense of the affinities between the sociology of knowl-edge and ideas of Dewey was essentially correct, but I must admit at the outset that the following pages only involve an analysis of the first of what should be a two-part analysis that would be required to establish the connection between Dewey and the sociology of knowledge.

The first step of the analysis, which requires concentrated attention, focuses on how the sociology of knowledge can be used to explain the conceptual map-building process of socialization that enables the culturally uninitiated child to participate in the adult world of meaning. It also involves a deliberately extended discussion of the practical implications of thinking within a sociology of knowledge framework. Since previous encounters with the sociology of knowledge seemed to generate a sense of ennui before the practical implications had been explored, a systematic attempt has been made to identify the analytical tools this framework makes available to classroom teachers and to explore, in concrete terms, the implications for teaching and curriculum reform.

The second step of analysis, which would have explored the connections between the sociology of knowledge and Dewey's epistemological position—his views on the relation between education and a democratic polity and his proposals for reforming schools in a manner that fosters a scientifically-oriented form of intelligence—could not be undertaken in any meaningful way until the first stage has been developed more fully. This book in no way represents an exhaustive treatment of the first stage, but it goes far enough in establishing the outline of a theory of education to suggest issues worth examining in the second stage of analysis.

The following attempt to expand the sociology of knowledge into a general theory of education immediately brings into focus a number of issues that suggest important continuities, as well as points of fundamental difference, with Dewey's philosophy. The sociology of knowledge (supplemented by insights of the more linguistically-oriented cultural anthropologists) brings into focus the connection between the epistemological categories of the culture reproduced through language and individual thought and behavior, the reality constituting and maintenance role of communication, the individual as an unconscious carrier of the culture's symbolic history, and the influence of culture on what the individual perceives to be the basic existential questions. Specifically the comparative mind is led to ask whether the epistemological assumptions underlying Dewey's view of thinking would stand up against the argument that thought is influenced, in part, by the cultural orientations embedded in language. Dewey's understanding of the relationship between communication, social renewal, and intelligence suggests important comparisons with the conservative role assigned to communication in Berger and Luckmann's *The Social Construction of Reality*. Dewey's way of locating the method of intelligence in an ontological framework of progressive change deserves to be compared with the cultural conservativism that emerges (as opposed to being advocated as an ideological position) from an examination of how socialization reproduces the tacit historical knowledge of a culture. The difference between Dewey's view of habit and the sociology of knowledge view of the natural attitude also draws attention. There is also a need to compare Dewey's views on teaching and curriculum reform with the recommendations derived from the sociology of knowledge. A study of George H. Mead's influence in the sociology of knowledge would help to clarify the continuities between Dewey's position, which was also influenced by Mead, and the sociology of knowledge. Clearly, the second stage of analysis could quickly overcome the first stage in terms of adding to our understanding of the theoretical foundations of education. But the first stage is needed to pose questions and establish a framework for comparative analysis. It also stands on its own in terms of establishing theoretical bases for educational reforms that address current cultural, political, and ecological problems.

In addition to the John Dewey Society, I owe a special debt to Salvatore D'Urso of the University of Queensland for his critical response to the first chapter and for the intellectual guidance he has given me through several years of correspondence. His "reading lists" have prodded me to move intellectually in directions he could not have anticipated; consequently, my expression of gratitude should not be interpreted to mean that he is in any way responsible for what I have done with his largess. I also wish to thank Phyllis Wells for the skill, patience, and cheerfulness she brought to the task of transforming my formidable handwriting into the typewritten page. Her assistance is particularly valued because she continued with the project even after I changed departmental affiliation.

1

The Educational Challenge of Modernization

The process of renegotiating basic aspects of our belief system has gone on throughout Western history but has accelerated in recent years under the pressure of modernization. This renegotiation process has also become more democratic. In some areas the renegotiation has been motivated by a greater sense of social justice and human dignity. The delegitimization of forms of authority that maintained sexist attitudes, as well as an increased awareness of dehumanized forms of work relationships and the crisis of our world view that no longer makes sense in an era of increased ecological understanding, has led to a renegotiation process where more democratically based forms of communicative competence have prevailed. These battles, however, have not been won entirely. Nor, for that matter, do we face a situation where the need for communicative competence on the part of the people will be reduced. The law of entropy, which states that the forms of energy available for human use are progressively transformed into nonusable states, means that fundamental aspects of our cultural maps (which are predicted on expansion rather than contraction of the supply of energy) will have to be renegotiated. This will cause a rethinking of basic cultural assumptions related, among others, to our notions about what constitutes human progress, the nature and purpose of work, the rights associated with individualism, the distribution of wealth, and our view of technology. Other aspects of our belief system have been opened to renegotiation by changes that have occurred in other areas of our belief system. The "right to life" issue, as well as issues relating to democratizing the workplace, are two prominent examples. Advances in technology and the struggle by special interest groups to impose their views on others have problematized other areas of our value system that previously were treated as taken-for-granted human rights. Technological innovation, combined with expansion of the influences of governmental power, has in recent years politicized many traditional rights of the individual. How much privacy is to be allowed in the era of the computer and how human rights can be protected from those who possess expert knowledge are two other areas that point to the need for communicative competence in an increasingly politicized world.

If we take communicative competence as a primary goal of public education that seems appropriate in an increasingly politicized world, the next task is to consider the implications of this goal for a theory of education. Communicative competence, a phrase borrowed from Jurgen Habermas's overly abstract formulation, can be understood most simply in terms of the individual's ability to negotiate meanings and purposes instead of passively accepting the social realities defined by others. Communicative competence requires, beyond individual facility in speech situations, a knowledge of relevant issues and the conceptual frameworks that influence our way of thinking. The unique contributions that public education can make to the student's communicative competence include: (1) providing an understanding of the cultural forces that foster change; (2) providing knowledge of cultural traditions that will enable students to exercise a judgment about those elements of the culture that are worth preserving; and (3) providing a method of thinking that enables students to see decisions in social life in terms of relationships, continuities, disjunctions, and trade-offs. In short, communicative competence can be understood as the outcome of being culturally literate, which I have described elsewhere as the ability to read or decode the taken-for-granted assumptions and conceptual categories that underlie the individual's world of experience.[1]

It is possible to obtain a clearer sense of how to formulate a theory of education that contributes to communicative competence by recognizing how people acquired the communicative competence necessary for the political transformation of deeply held beliefs that seemed increasingly inappropriate in a democratic society. The process of relativizing traditional forms of authority that maintained sexist and racist attitudes involved the process of making explicit taken-for-granted beliefs and social habits. In effect, the ability to recognize that sexist and racist attitudes were embedded at the deepest level of our conceptual maps led to an examination of the basic assumptions on which our natural attitudes were based. The process of negotiation involved both the levels of social practice and the deeper cultural codes that dictated our patterns of thought and feeling and set limits on what we were able to imagine. Negotiating those aspects of the belief system that maintained a taken-for-granted attitude toward sexist and racist social practices was difficult and in some ways only partially successful. But the process of negotiating a new basis of understanding did go on, and what is more important for those who may think the goal of communicative competence is abstract and unrelated to public education, the schools were increasingly involved in developing the student's communicative competence in dealing with sexist and racist attitudes.

The basic relationships that must be understood by educators concerned with fostering communicative competence is the role that language (or communication, in the broadest sense) plays in reproducing in individual consciousness the conceptual maps we associate with culture. In effect, the educator must understand the different dynamics that operate when communication transmits and reinforces taken-for-granted beliefs (such as sexist attitudes) and when communication makes explicit the assumptions and patterns of thought, thus enabling the individual to obtain the distance necessary for critical reflection. This understanding will require a theoretical framework that focuses on the interaction of the cultural belief system, the role of language and communication, and human consciousness. The sociology of knowledge developed by Alfred Schutz, Peter Berger, and Thomas Luckmann seems especially powerful as a conceptual framework for understanding the social formation of consciousness and for illuminating the "moves" in the language game of socialization that contribute to the individual's communicative competence.

At first glance, it might appear that basing education on a theoretical framework that increases the individual's awareness of the binding power of cultural belief contributes to the relativizing process discussed earlier. However, basing the educational process on insights derived from the sociology of knowledge framework of Schutz, Berger, and Luckmann does not lead to the narcissistic and self-indulgent form of individualism that has concerned many social critics. By emphasizing the social origins of our patterns of thinking, a sociological approach to education puts a renewed emphasis on understanding our beliefs and the language systems that both transmit and sustain these beliefs. In effect, the incorporation of this perspective in classroom practice deepens our understanding of what John Dewey called the "social character of intelligence." This understanding may lead to relativizing certain taken-for-granted beliefs (including the idea of self-contained individuals), but it will not reinforce the cultural tendency to view everything as relative to the individual's perspective. The individual is unconsciously controlled by cultural traditions in many ways that are not recognized by either the technocratic, neo-Marxist, or neoromantic theorists of education, who have reworked with minor variation, but not gone beyond Enlightenment assumptions about the nature of individualism, change, and the rational process.

By keeping in focus the connection between culture, communication, and consciousness, it should be possible to develop a theory of education that recognizes the tension between the existential freedom (and responsibility) of the individual and the claims of tradition and society. This tension is essential to exercising communicative competence, as the formulation of new meanings and conventions involves the individual both as an existential being and as a carrier and guardian of worthwhile cultural traditions. Theorists of education, who contributed to relativizing traditional beliefs, overlooked the fact that the renewal of cultural beliefs and practices also involves making judgments about what must be preserved as part of the collective heritage.

The task in the following chapters is to develop a theory of education that will add to our understanding of how education influences the consciousness of the student, and of the power that teachers exercise over whether the process of socialization limits the student to the taken-for-granted beliefs of modern culture or expands the student's knowledge in a manner that makes informed choice a possibility. This involves identifying certain insights in the sociology of knowledge that will help us see more clearly the "moves" in the language game of socialization that go on in the classroom. By thinking metaphorically of socialization as a language game, we can think of the different "moves" available to the teacher. This should help to challenge the fatalism that often characterizes our view of educational reform, as well as challenge the educational technocrat who is attempting, through the development of highly systematized techniques and learning packages, to reform education by taking effective decision-making out of the hands of the teacher. Before we begin this task, however, it is essential to examine the connection between the relativizing characteristics of modernization and the growing political significance of communicative competence. It would also be useful to put in clearer focus how such contemporary educational reformers as the liberal-technocrats, neoromantics, and neo-Marxists strengthen the modernizing tendencies of society. Why these groups have not adopted a more problematic attitude toward the educational implications of modernization is an important question. A better grasp of the political implications of modernization and the areas of silence that characterize contemporary theories of educational reform will help put in perspective the contribution that the sociology of knowledge can make to strengthening our understanding of the educational process.

MODERNIZATION AND THE RELATIVIZING OF AUTHORITY

It is difficult to discuss modernization without appearing to make a value judgment. For many people, the term itself carries the powerful connotation of social progress; while for others the term suggests a mindless pursuit of change and the mesmerism of materialistic consumer values. In spite of the partisanship that surrounds the term, I would like to discuss an important characteristic of modernization without taking sides in the debate over how to judge it. The characteristic I would like to put in sharper focus relates to the relativizing of traditional forms of cultural authority. This process of relativizing the various forms of authority that give social life its predictability and continuity with the past creates the liminal social and conceptual space that allows for the redefinition of meanings and social practices. Specifically, I want to examine how the relativizing of the foundations of taken-for-granted beliefs leads to politicizing more areas of everyday life and to identify the ideas and values that contribute to this propensity of modern society. The argument that formal education should contribute to the student's communicative competence is based essentially on an understanding of these connections.

In order to understand the political implications of the relativizing process it is necessary to clarify the nature of cultural authority in regulating thought and social behavior. The authority that culture exercises over us can best be understood if we keep in mind Hannah Arendt's distinction between authority and authoritarian forms of power and violence. As she states, "authority precludes the use of external means of coercion; where force is used, authority itself has failed."[2] Put another way, this form of authority is internalized in such a way that the person under its sway experiences it as part of the natural order of things. This particular view of authority is particularly useful in understanding the hold that culture has over us. As the medium through which we move, culture provides the information codes that regulate our patterns of thought, body language, use of space, social interaction, rituals, and economic and political systems. But most of the information codes that provide the blueprints for how to think and act in specific situations are both learned and experienced at a tacit level. In describing the tacit authority of the information codes that make up our culture, Edward Hall suggested we think of the cultural controls over thought and social behavior as similar to the principle of negative feedback. To paraphrase Hall, as long as information codes of the culture are followed, the individual "is completely unaware of the fact that there is a system of controls."[3] That we are unconscious of most of our cultural knowledge, a point we shall examine later, accounts for not being aware of the authority that culture has over us; thus we have the irony of people thinking that their "rationally"-based decisions reflect their individual autonomy when, in fact, they are under the authority of the language systems (discursive, spatial, body, etc.) of the culture that makes thought and communication possible.

Our modern notion of the autonomous individual leads us to view authority as something external to the individual, and thus it is difficult to recognize how much we are under the authority of cultural traditions. The degree to which our patterns of thought and social behavior reproduce the traditions of the past is not the primary question for us, although the ensuing discussion of how the relativizing process gives communicative competence a special political significance will make sense only as we keep in mind the tacit and pervasive nature of the authority of traditional culture. Our primary focus is on the tendencies within modernizing cultures to relativize the conceptual foundations of culture and, in the process, give political power to those individuals and social groups who are able to exploit the liminal space by using language to create a new conceptual basis for authority. As the relativizing process goes on in one area of our thought and social behavior, we continue to be influenced by traditional forms of cultural authority in other areas. The feminist movement, as well as the attempt to shift to the metric system, serve as two examples of changes being negotiated in the midst of cultural continuities. The changes themselves may later become the part of culture that exerts its tacit influence over us.

The relativizing of culture is fostered by a number of ideas and values, which we shall examine shortly, and this phenomenon is experienced in different ways. The most common example of the relativizing process is the questioning of taken-for-granted beliefs. As the beliefs and social behaviors are made explicit and examined in a critical manner they lose their traditional hold on us. The relativizing process may also result from the displacement of traditional taken-for-granted beliefs by fresh ideas, as occurs in the changes in educational ideas and social mores. For example, the concern that students acquire a higher level of competency in basic subject areas led to forgetting our previous concerns about the self-realization of the student. The authority of the neoromantic ideology, which produced powerful images just a few years ago, no longer influences our thought at the taken-for-granted level. The relativizing of traditional authority can also occur by not socializing the individual to areas of culture shared by previous generations. The authority that certain political ideas, such as the Bill of Rights, has exercised over our most basic political impulses is eroded when the individual has not been exposed to these ideas. In not possessing a knowledge of the political language, and the tacit assumptions of that tradition of ideas, the individual is not likely to possess a set of taken-for-granted beliefs pertaining to the importance of maintaining civil liberties, nor be able to establish a position on more rational grounds. The lack of knowledge and exposure to the collective traditions that enable the individual to share in the collective memory will not lead to the individual being influenced by the authority of this area of the culture.

As taken-for-granted beliefs are made explicit and are challenged, there is a moment in social and conceptual time when the individual experiences the temporary openness of liminal space. As the Dutch anthropologist Arnold van Gennep uses the concept, liminality designates those moments in cultural transition where the individual is "betwixt and between" established patterns of thought and behavior.[4] While he uses the concept of liminality to investigate the transitions from one role or station in life to another, the concept can also be used to highlight the brief period of openness that follows the relativizing of taken-for-granted authority. Problematizing our taken-for-granted beliefs toward the hierarchical organization of work both frees the individual from authority, as Arendt uses the term, and creates the liminal space that makes it possible to define the work relationship in new ways. To cite another example, questioning the taken-for-granted beliefs pertaining to the role of women in raising children created the liminal space where a whole set of previously established relationships, values and ideas could be redefined.

The liminal space that follows the relativizing process gives language a special political significance. In being "betwixt and between" accepted definitions that will serve as the basis of social experience, new definitions can be presented, and the conceptual foundations of authority renegotiated. Prior to the relativizing process communication performs the conservative political function of reinforcing traditional ways. As tradition is disrupted, the political role of communication changes; the liminality of the social situation provides the potential for a transition to new ways of thinking and acting. This moment of openness gives those who possess the linguistic ability to name "what is" in new ways, and convince others to accept their definitions, a basic form of political power. In effect the liminality gives language, and those who either can use it effectively or control how it is used, a political significance that it does not have in more traditional cultures. In cultures where meanings and definitions are not being continually renegotiated people do not have to possess the range of explicit knowledge essential for talking about how reality is to be defined. Social contexts play a more significant role in the communication of meaning, with tacit forms of understandings providing the basis of an integrated social life. The communication between members of the traditional Ibo village in Chinua Achebe's, *Things Fall Apart*, serves to strengthen the bonds of community; theoretical forms of knowledge and a disposition toward problematizing taken-for-granted beliefs are notably absent.

In suggesting that the liminal spaces in thought and social practice give discourse a powerful political role in establishing the conceptual foundations for new forms of authority, I am not suggesting that everybody is equally capable of participating in the renegotiation process. The disruption of routines and taken-for-granted beliefs can provide a sense of liminality that is experienced by some as psychologically disorienting, and they will not see it as an opportunity to participate in a community process of renegotiation. They are more likely to be reactionary, in the sense of wanting to return to traditional practices, or to follow the authoritarian who will give them a new basis for belief. Some people may not be able to respond to the political challenge of liminality because they have not experienced the conceptual disruption of their taken-for-granted world. Others may not be able to participate effectively in the renegotiation process because they lack the conceptual foundations essential for communicative competence. In order to reconceptualize the organization of work, for example, the individual must possess a complex body of knowledge that will provide a basis for an historical and comparative perspective, an understanding of how other significant groups think about the work process (including their taken-for-granted assumptions), and an ability to think theoretically about the relation of work to other aspects of social life: economic, political, existential, and ecological. As we observe different social groups challenging governmental policies we can see that their communicative competence, which is often considerable, is not based on the limited language code of taken-for-granted knowledge, nor is it acquired quickly as a response to a perceived political threat. The conceptual foundations are much deeper and broader, and thus are not acquired in a superficial manner. How education can contribute to developing the knowledge and analytical skills necessary for communicative importance will be explored more fully in sections of the book dealing with teaching and curriculum.

ELEMENTS OF THE IDEOLOGY OF MODERNISM

Is communicative competence an ability that everybody should possess or is it sufficient to look to experts as the group responsible for restoring the fabric of culture as it becomes disrupted? The answer to the question, which has implications for how we view the purpose of schools, depends in part on whether the reader possesses a commitment to a democratic form of polity. The politicizing of ideas, values, and social practices that results from the breakdown of authority generally has broad social implications that exceed the specialized approach to problem-solving that characterize experts educated in narrow areas of specialization. There is also the issue of whether the people affected by a decision should participate in its formulation, a position to which I find myself sympathetic. The alternative often involves decision making by experts who think about the problem in an abstract language code that discounts the importance of fully understanding the cultural context, and who often do not have to live with the consequences of their efforts. The answer to the question of how widely communicative competence should be shared is also related to whether the relativizing of cultural traditions is perceived to be a limited phenomena that can be dealt with by a relatively few informed individuals or an increasingly significant characteristic of modern life. The question cannot be answered in specific terms by current social science research, but a more general understanding of the scope of the phenomena can be obtained by identifying the ideas and values that contribute to the relativizing process. In considering the scope of the influence of ideas and values that underpin the modernizing ideology, we might ask whether a modern culture possesses a counter ideology that restricts the areas of culture that can be relativized by this "progressive" pattern of thinking. Even though I will not make the issue a central focus of the subsequent discussion it should become quite clear as I identify the essential conceptual elements of a modern way of thinking that ideological alternatives to the modernizing process simply do not exist in any creditable form. To say this does not mean to imply that the liberal ideas underlying the modernizing ideology are not being challenged by an increasing number of serious thinkers.

In identifying, in summary fashion, the conceptual traits associated with the modern mode of consciousness one should keep in mind that the discussion is not intended to cover new ground. There is already a rich literature on the theme of modernization. My approach is the more limited one of helping an educational audience that seems to have taken modernization as its "manifest destiny" bring into focus how the ideas and values associated with being modern contribute to creating the liminal conceptual and social-cultural spaces that follow the relativizing process. In effect, the chief purpose is to call attention to the educational implications of a culture that increasingly politicizes the foundations of authority used to legitimitize the routines of everyday life.

Overviews are always dangerous, and in order to avoid one possible source of confusion it is important to recognize that what I term "society" is composed of many different groups who ground their symbolic worlds differently. Some groups possess ways of thinking deeply rooted in the culture of their ancestors; other groups ground their view of reality in religious beliefs and at the same time attempt to regulate their everyday lives in accordance with the pattern of thought that characterizes the dominant, modern culture. By recognizing the array of different belief systems, the way belief systems interpenetrate each other, as well as their adversarial relationships, it is easier to understand that the ideas and values associated with modern culture are not held universally. The spread of a modern mode of consciousness by elite groups, such as experts, artists, intellectuals, and image shapers who serve the interests of the technoconsumer sectors of society, often involves conflict and domination. But unlike Japanese and Islamic cultures which have maintained viable intellectual and religious traditions that support resisting modernization, cultural groups in this society risk being seen as pariahs if they reject modernization.

The modernizing mode of consciousness, which must also be understood as a Westernizing form of hegemonic culture, possesses the following traits that separate it from the patterns of thought associated with traditional cultures. Basic to the break with traditional patterns of thought was the way change came to be viewed by groups of progressive thinkers in western Europe during the late sixteenth and early seventeenth centuries. The acceptance that change is normal, even desirable when guided by rational thought, went against the view held in most traditional cultures that change represents an undesirable disruption. As Robert Bellah observed, the new attitude toward change not only legitimatized breaking the continuities that bound the present to the past but also created a problem of identity. As Bellah stated:

> The notion that consciously directioned change is a primary human responsibility presents enormous problems for social as well as psychic and perhaps even biological balance. It seems to violate one of the cardinal requirements of organized action of any sort, namely the need for continuity, for stability of orientation—in a word, for identity. . . . The great problem for the modern conception of change, then, was how to integrate it with a conception of identity, a conception traditionally provided by religion.[5]

As change became part of the natural attitude toward everyday life, a new attitude toward authority had to be formulated. Authority, as the collective pressure to preserve traditional patterns and beliefs, gave way to the idea that the individual could be the center of authority. This involved reviving the Greek idea that reason is the highest expression of authority. But the rational process that gave the person power to overturn tradition and direct the course of change was not viewed, in its modern reformulation, as a means of apprehending eternal verities. Rationalism, as Friederich Nietzsche and, more recently, Alvin Gouldner have pointed out,[6] has been given the mission of overturning traditional beliefs. It has become associated, according to Arnold Gehlen, with a sense of "omnipotence" that has led to what he sees as the characteristic mode of operation of the modern spirit: "attacking the foundations, manipulating the central components, reconsidering the originating assumptions of whatever one is dealing with."[7]

This sense of the power of rational thought did not entirely shape the modern view of individualism. Self-expression and, later in our time, "self-realization" became essential aspects of authentic individualism. In the artistic world this was expressed as the creative power of imagination. Daniel Bell identified the consequences of the modern view of individualism when he wrote:

> The chiliasm of modern man, the mainspring of his life, is the megalomania of self-infinitization. In consequence, the modern hubris is the refusal to accept limits and to continually reach out; and the modern world is *beyond*—to go always beyond, beyond mortality, beyond tragedy, beyond culture.[8]

This refusal to accept limits, combined with the sense of agency associated with rational thought, led to a fundamental shift in the way in which modern consciousness understood the nature of time. The sense of time and human activities became intertwined in such a way that change came to be seen as the expression of progress. The rapid development of technological innovation during the latter part of the eighteenth century and the industrial revolution of the nineteenth century strengthened the idea of unlimited abundance. Darwin's theory of evolution provided a powerful metaphor for understanding social "evolution" and progress giving the new myth a sense of scientific respectability. The convergence of intellectual activities in philosophy and the emerging social sciences, as well as in scientific understanding and technology, served to strengthen the element of modern consciousness that viewed tradition as an obstacle to further progress. The temporal orientation of the new consciousness was in the present and future; the past represented the "dark ages," superstition, and an unhealthy form of constraint.

The belief in progress led to a fundamental misunderstanding of the hold that tradition has over people's pattern of thought and social behavior. The sense of atomistic individualism, the power for self-direction found in the exercise of reason, and the view that change is a progressive movement beyond the past led to the incredibly naive belief that people could free themselves from their past. In the political realm this was expressed through the idea of revolution, which was supposed to involve a clear break with the past and a new beginning. Marx speaks of the "beginning of human history" that is to follow revolution. On a more individual level, the sense of individual agency, which is still seen as free of the influence of tradition, is expressed in the natural attitude toward individual thought and creativity. The phrase "autonomous individual" reflects the myth of being free of the past. In the technological realm the emphasis on the "new" communicates the same modern attitude. When one considers the ways in which the present is shaped by the past (how language reproduces the epistemological categories of the past, the historical continuities of events, behaviors, and ideas, and the shaping influence of the past on individual identity—to cite the more obvious examples), one can only wonder how people were able to maintain the mythic belief in the face of such overwhelming evidence to the contrary.[9] The indifference, if not hostility, has led to the view that ignorance of the past is a virtue, a sign that one is taking control of one's life by directing it toward personally meaningful goals. Ignorance of traditions thus goes beyond relativizing traditional culture in the way that is characteristic of critical inquiry; without the language to name the past, it simply ceases to have any reality to the individual.

Though the analysis is by no means complete, the last characteristic I want to discuss relates to the secularized world view of modern consciousness. Secularization can be understood at several levels. Its original meaning denoted the removal of territory or property from ecclesiastical authority. This sense of the term relates to the separation of church and state as we know it today. At another level, secularization refers to a fundamental change in consciousness. Max Weber referred to the secularization of Western thought as the "disenchantment" of our world view. He used another interesting metaphor, the "iron cage," to describe the progressive rationalization he saw displacing religious belief.

Segmenting social and psychic life into separate domains became a distinguishing characteristic of modern consciousness. The privatizing of religious belief meant that religion became separated from other areas of cultural life, a unique departure in the history of the world's cultures. Commenting on the shift in consciousness, Lucian Goldmann, the Marxist historian and social critic, wrote:

> By the eighteenth century the area of bourgeois life occupied by rational thought and action had grown so far that the *nature* of the question had altered. It was no longer a question of the place to be assigned to reason in a life built on faith, but rather of what place there could be for faith within a world vision grounded on reason.[10]

Daniel Bell has observed that religions have traditionally provided a "set of coherent answers to the core existential questions that confront every human group."[11] Accepting the secularized world as a social convention has not necessarily relegated religious belief to the subjective domain of the individual. Within this secular world, civic and political religions have emerged. But because they are based on beliefs in the nature of reason, individual self-realization, progress, and the power of the state and political party, they are seen as expressions of the spirit of modernism rather than as new forms of religious belief.[12] But secularization has changed how we view the moral foundations of public policy decisions. Moral absolutes that previously could be grounded in religious teachings gave way to natural laws governing supply and demand in the economic sphere and to utilitarianism in the area of public policy. In effect, secularization enabled modern consciousness to separate morality from both the economic and political domains. This relativizing of the moral order led to a progressive dependence upon the quantification of behavior as a means of determining the basis of social consensus. Counting votes, taking public opinion polls, and adjusting policy decisions to shifts in public attitudes reflect today's natural attitude toward using the utilitarian principle of the greatest good for the greatest number as the basis for determining policy issues. The privatizing of religious belief has thus relativized the moral basis of public policy, but it has not provided a check on the growing power of the state to extend its control over the life of the individual or the state's tendency to justify its extension of power on positivistic grounds.

The pattern of thought that underlies modernization is essentially messianic in overturning every fixed position, regardless of how great of a cultural achievement it represents. Yet the achievements of this mode of consciousness are themselves in continual danger of becoming a tradition that must be overturned by fresh expressions of progressive, modern thought. Irving Howe identified the essential characteristic and source of energy of this mode of consciousness: "The dilemma that modernism must always struggle but never quite triumphs, and then, after a time, must struggle in order not to triumph."[13] This tendency to relativize all traditions, even its own, does not mean that modern consciousness does not have its own value orientation. In the area of technology and consumerism, the modern spirit is expressed in terms of a continual demand for new inventions and social techniques that are cost effective, efficient, and marketable. In the public policy sector, utilitarian principles provide the guidelines for maximizing the values of freedom and equality in daily life. This is increasingly expressed in a populist form of politics that threatens traditional civic guarantees. In literature and the therapeutic sciences there has been a shift from "truth to sincerity, from the search for objective law to a desire for authentic response," to quote Irving Howe. Commenting on the consequences of this shift in conceptual orientation, Howe directs our attention to the darker side of the signal values of modern consciousness. Sincerity, for example, can become "the last-ditch defense for men without belief, and in its name absolutes can be toppled, morality dispensed, and intellectual systems dissolved."[14]

The expression of modernism in all sectors of public and individual life has produced important material and social benefits, as well as unleased sources of energy that threaten to swamp the gains that have been made. The paradoxical nature of this relativizing, modern culture cannot simply be dismissed with the view that we can substitute an alternative form of culture. We cannot change the conceptual maps in the same way we exchange one commodity for another. Nor can we embrace modernization uncritically by accepting the idea that it is the embodiment of social progress. But at this point, we can recognize that the culture of relativism, which the modern mode of consciousness produces, has important implications for how we educate the youth of society.

MODERNIZING IDEOLOGY OF EDUCATIONAL REFORMERS

The ideas of educational critics and reformers serve as an important example of how widely the relativizing ideas and values of modernization are taken-for-granted. To many critics of the schools, the argument that schools are a modernizing force must sound ludicrous indeed. The conventional wisdom, shared by liberal and leftist educational critics, is that schools are fundamentally conservative institutions. With justification, they can point to fundamental structures of authority, as well as certain elements of the curriculum, that reflect the conservative nature of schools. But much of the evidence used to link schools with conservativism—competitive individualism and the meritocratic nature of the grading and placement systems—reflects the values of classical liberalism on which technoconsumer society depends.

In order to grasp the connection between schools and the culture of relativism it is necessary to set aside the conventional wisdom, along with the recipe analyses and prescriptions that have created a growing sense of ennui for the reader of educational literature. This can be done by recognizing that what we think and experience is influenced, to a significant degree, by the cultural maps or schemas we carry around in our heads. In effect, these cultural maps represent historically grounded message systems that cause thoughts and feelings to be organized in ways that reflect the categories, assumptions, and patterns of thinking acquired through socialization to the culture's way of organizing reality. Critics who have argued that schools are reactionary and conservative institutions have not recognized that their analyses are largely conditioned by the modernizing ideology; to admit this would involve abandoning the myth that rational, critical thought reflects the culturally uncontaminated higher qualities of a commitment to truth and social progress. The sense of the natural order of things (a feeling of taken-for-granted belief) has desensitized both educational critics and mainstream educators from recognizing their ideological bias. In effect, those groups have failed to recognize the relativizing influence of schools on traditional culture for the simple reason that their natural attitude was shaped by the ideology that underlies the modernizing elements of our culture.

Within the educational establishment, many interest groups impose conflicting demands on public schools. But it is possible to identify one group that has exerted a powerful influence on the direction of educational policy and classroom practice and two other groups that have served as vocal critics. These groups are often critical of one another and appear on the surface to have different social and educational goals. But when we examine how their ideas and values reflect a modernizing cultural orientation, their criticisms of one another's position appear analogous to three different arguments on how to make the train they are all riding go even faster. It is not an argument about changing directions or whether the train is worth being on in the first place. Just as the train moves inexorably down the track, these three groups—liberal-technocratic educational reformers, neoromantic advocates of progressive free schools, and neo-Marxist critics—are following the same cultural map and are committed to the same trajectory of cultural evolution. In identifying their basic value orientation we shall be mapping essential characteristics of our modernizing form of consciousness.

The main apostles of modernizing consciousness are the liberal-technocratic educators who operate within the mainstream of the educational establishment, but their influence over public schools appears to come from the dominant position they hold in teacher-training institutions. At the college level, liberal-technocratic educators train prospective teachers in efficient management techniques, generate a continual stream of theories to improve classroom instruction and administrative control of the school, conduct research to validate their knowledge claims, and produce curriculum materials that give the appearance of individualizing the learning of information that is increasingly one-dimensional. This group is supported by liberal-technocratic professionals in state departments of education and federally-funded research and development institutes committed to disseminating to classroom teachers a steady stream of innovative techniques and teaching materials. Classroom teachers are increasingly being educated to the language code that reproduces the liberal-technocratic way of thinking; and this way of thinking is reinforced through the professional literature they encounter in the school, as well as through the new techniques and materials continually presented as an opportunity for professional growth. As public schools reflect the syncretism that results from the intermingling of cultures in American society, it would be incorrect to assume that all classroom teachers, professors of education, and educational bureaucrats subscribe to the more extreme expression of technocratic thinking that has emerged on the educational scene in the last few years. But even the less "progressive" educators share the same cultural assumptions about rationality, progress, and an anthropocentric universe that serve as the foundation of liberal-technocratic thinking.

Liberal-technocratic educators possess a high commitment to improving the effectiveness of classroom instruction, which they see as necessitating more effective teacher control over classrooms. Consequently, teaching techniques and packaged learning materials like "Direct Instruction" reflect a hierarchical authority structure and appear to support a meritocratic process of social stratification that supposedly reflects the student's level of ability. To the neoromantic advocates of the humanist-free school and the neo-Marxist educational critics, the liberal-technocratic educators, who are directing the main course of educational innovation and reform, appear as conservative, authoritarian, and at odds with any social change along humanistic lines. However, one can argue that this view is basically wrong on all counts. The liberal-technocratic educators are not defenders of tradition (unless one wants to argue that the modernizing mode of consciousness is the tradition being conserved), nor are they advocates of the status quo. On the question of authoritarianism there is a real difference between neoromantic and liberal-technocratic educators though one could argue that the followers of Rousseau practice a form of authoritarianism that is more difficult to see and thus more difficult to resist. For example, people who do not subscribe to the neoromantic's views on the educational value of free expression and equality in the classroom would encounter an authoritarian form of hostility that reflects the tendency to think of dissenters as political enemies. Neo-Marxists are grounded in the same traditions of thought that lead the liberal-technocrat to give theory a preeminent role in directing practice. When compared to other objections to their position, the criticism of liberal-technocratic educators as enemies of humanistically-oriented social change is most ironic especially when we recognize that their basic pattern of thought reflects the most extreme formulation of the humanistic view of man as a rational being.

As Raymond Callahan noted in *Education and the Cult of Efficiency*, liberal-technocrat educators have been in the forefront of American educational reform for decades. The development of intelligence testing, theories of school management, and the use of behavioral techniques in the classroom stand out as their more prominent achievements. But in the last few years, their efforts have produced in rapid succession a near-overwhelming series of educational administrative and instructional techniques: management by objectives, competency-based instruction, data-based decision-making, "Direct Instruction," "Distar," and assertive discipline. What is common to educational innovations is the mind set that reflects the assumptions and categories of thought that are fundamental to a modernizing mode of consciousness.

A key element of this mode of thought is the status given to the power of abstract ideas expressed in the form of theory. Most of us have been so conditioned by the assumptions of modernization that this statement fails to generate much excitement or even a sense of puzzlement. The belief that abstract ideas should guide social experience has become basic to our natural attitude toward everyday life; and with this idea has come the acceptance of the unique social role of those in possession of expert knowledge.[15] In the hands of liberal-technicist educators, theory has become the talisman for centralizing authority over the decision-making process and increasing the efficiency of control and predictability. This has been achieved through the development by experts of systems (e.g., "Distar," "Direct Instruction," behavior modification techniques, etc.) that are to be used in classrooms throughout the country. What is unique to the modernizing process is the way in which this approach discounts the importance of commonsense experiences and tacit forms of knowledge acquired by the teacher in a specific cultural contexts.

Another key element of the liberal-technocratic educator's pattern of thought is the belief that change, based on abstract ideas and theory, is progressive. This part of the liberal-humanist tradition leads, within the field of education, to a generally held state of mind in which change is automatically associated with progress and thus is not only expected but seen as a sign of a healthy state of affairs. The justification that change is progressive is found in the use of measurement to validate increasing levels of efficiency and predictability. Data that serve as evidence of increased efficiency thus become tied to the utilitarian principle of providing the greatest good for the greatest number (i.e., data are used to settle moral issues on the equally abstract basis of serving the "common good").

A primary objective of liberal-technocrat educators is to rationalize both the classroom and the school as part of a social system. As their mode of thinking serves as a carrier of the form of rationalism that Max Weber associated with modernization, it would be useful to clarify how their activities contribute to the relativizing of cultural tradition. On the surface, it would seem that substituting rationally formulated procedures and systems of action for behavior based on a mixture of personal understanding and tacit cultural norms shared by members of the same language community would further integrate society into a common order. This appears to be the opposite of a relativizing process. But as Peter Berger and Hansfried Kellner point out, when the rationalizing of behavior and social practice breaks down or leads to unanticipated consequences, the people who have accepted the top-down organization of their experience will be less able to understand the problems associated with the failed system because the rationalizing process has disassociated them from their cultural roots.[16] The relativizing of traditional culture occurs at both ends of the rationalizing process. The initial rationalization involves disrupting the legitimating and holding power of traditional beliefs and practices; when the rationalized procedure or system fails, the people experience a further disintegration of their world view as they attempt to go back to old values and thought patterns that have lost their plausibility.

One source of liberal-technoratic educators' power to relativize traditional culture is in their ability to superimpose their language code on the language that is instrumental in sustaining local patterns of thought. If it is recognized that the life style of a community is sustained by patterns of communication and the epistemological code embedded in the language, it then becomes easier to see the political consequences of introducing a language that carries a different conceptual map. Liberal-technocratic educators have not been entirely succssful in imposing their language code on classroom teachers although this is not because of their lack of effort. But their partial success in getting teachers to talk in the language of behavioral objectives, performance indicators, inputs, adjustment, data-based decision-making, educational product, and the like, suggests that teachers' language, and thus their conceptual maps, is being modernized.

An example of how the language of the liberal-technocratic educator both relativizes (delegitimatizes) and creates a new form of dependency can be seen in a memorandum sent out of a school district office instructing teachers on how to think and write about "behavioral objectives." The memorandum begins with this statement: "In order for any objective to be considered measurable it should be derived from a goal statement and must have at least five components clearly defined." The teacher is then told that "the trick is to determine whether or not the

objective is written in terms that one can see, touch, taste, feel, or smell."
Without apologies or even token deference to the traditional values being
set aside, the real shift that the writer of the memorandum wants to make
in the teacher's conceptual framework is stated: "The verb is the key word
in the objective. If it describes a concrete, observable behavior like
'count,' 'list,' 'sort,' then you are on your way to a measurable performance. *However, if the verb is more abstract, like 'knows,' 'understands,'
'appreciates,' then you will probably never come to earth. . . .*"[17] This
memorandum is not unique in that it has no historical significance of its
own. It is simply a typical example of the liberal-technocratic pattern of
thinking. It is cited solely for the purpose of providing an example of the
political nature of language and what happens to traditional educational
values when the language of technicism is imposed on the classroom
teacher. The language introduces the one-dimensional reality of positivism where reality must be understood only in measurable terms. More
important, the language has no roots in the local context; consequently,
it can express neither the historically-grounded experience of the people
who are to use it, nor does it take into account the complex interplay of
psychological, linguistic, moral, and subjective elements that are part of
the teacher's social world. The language of liberal-technocrat thought,
which the quotation reflects, adheres to an important principle underlying
the historical development of the liberal and technocratic traditions that
gradually fused together in the late nineteenth century, namely that words
(*freedom, equality, individualism*, key liberal metaphors and *measurement, efficiency, system*, key technocrat metaphors) are to be understood
as culture free and are to have the same meaning regardless of cultural
context.

The modernizing culture reflected in the language of the liberal-
technocrat is aptly described by Daniel Bell's phrase of "gray on gray";
as this is a world that lacks existential and historical reference points,
teachers have both consciously and unconsciously resisted wholesale
acceptance of the world view implicit in the language of educational
reform. But they have not been totally unaffected, nor have students
escaped the influence of liberal-technocratic thought. When people crit-
icize public schools for being traditional and conservative (both words
tend to be used in the pejorative sense), they usually ignore the shaping
influence the school's covert curriculum has on the student's natural attitude toward time and space, as well as other essential elements of the
student's conceptual map.

As a result of dominating the direction of educational reform for the
last three decades, the liberal-technocratic pattern of thought is firmly
embedded as the covert curriculum of the school. This pattern of thought,
to reiterate, equates abstract thought with power, organizes experiences
into component parts, views the reorganization of components into new
systems as essential for asserting rational control, determines success on

the basis of efficiency, which can be measured, and views change as the normal state of affairs. This pattern of thought, elements of which reach deep into the early formative stages of Western history, is reproduced through the epistemological orientation of the teacher and curriculum materials. It is also reproduced through the structuring of school routines. To identify the essential elements is like drawing up a list of characteristics associated with the modernizing mode of consciousness that has carried to an extreme the evolution of the rational tradition started by the early Greek philosophers. Teaching students to think abstractly in a manner that eliminated the tension between thought and the context of their life world would be at the top of the list. Learning to think in the abstract, to associate progress with the formulation of new ideas, and to recognize the legitimating power of expert knowledge are essential to success for those students who are to attain the educational system's highest credentials. Not all students are able to discount experience when it does not correspond to pronouncements of theorists and experts; students who for one reason or another (not all of which can be viewed as heroic acts of resistance) cannot learn to think in the manner dictated by the aspect of the liberal-technocratic culture will find themselves tracked into lower-status occupational areas where abstract thought is not required.

In contrast to the traditional view of a liberalizing form of education that taught students to think more holistically about their cultural traditions, the covert curriculum of the school conditions students to accept crucial aspects of the liberal-technocratic mind set, such as the proclivity to segment reality into component parts. Organizing the curriculum into discrete units helps to establish the students' taken-for-granted attitude toward dividing experience into atomistic units that can be viewed as self-contained. History can be viewed as separate from biology and mathematics as a discrete area of inquiry that has nothing to do with the social sciences or humanities. The learning packages that are used in the elementary grades further increase the tendency toward segmenting knowledge. The segmenting of learning experiences, within the context of the school, also serves to condition students to another aspect of the liberal-technocratic mind set: to accept change in the cognitive and social realms as natural. The school environment does not leave the impression that change is *sui generis* or under the control of the student. Moving from one classroom to the next, which involves a constant change in acquaintances and social relationships, conditions students to accept change as part of an organized social system and to view this system, like the political state, as under the control of the purposive rational thought of experts.

Critics who identify schools as conservative institutions tend to over-emphasize the significance of authoritarian teachers and such practices as having students salute the flag. While authoritarianism and jingoism are important issues, they have little bearing on the larger question of whether schools are to be viewed as conservative institutions in need of being reconstructed along more liberal and modern lines. The curriculum in public schools already possesses such a high degree of contemporaneousness, which is of course essential in mathematics and the sciences, that only the more serious (and college-bound) students are likely to encounter literature that upholds more traditional values and to encounter questions about the human condition that have been asked throughout Western history. Nor are the more typical students likely, even in the freemarket environment of student electives, to encounter in any intellectually serious manner a culture not based on a technological world view or a consumer orientation to existential needs. One can only wonder what the critics of schools would propose as the alternative to what they see as the school's conservative grip on students' minds, and whether their solutions would simply lead to an acceleration of the modernizing and relativizing influence of the schools.

In recent years, two groups of critics have developed extended criticisms of public education. The neo-Marxists have generated the more significant line of analysis, while the neoromantic followers of Rousseau have developed an alternative approach to educational practice. Before taking up the question of the educational implications of the relativizing of traditional culture, it is necessary to clarify how the ideologies of neoromantic educators and the neo-Marxists contribute to the relativizing process.

One of the ironies of the recent alternative-free school movement is that the romantic tradition of thought used to justify freeing the child from adult constraints was originally formulated, in part, as a response to the dehumanization of the modernizing process of industrialization; however, the classroom practice of the romantic ideology contributes to the very value orientation that underlies the modern culture. The alternative-free schools that generated such hope in the 1960s reflected the recurrent appeal that the image of recovering a state of innocence has for American educational reformers. In the earlier phase of the progressive education movement, Freud provided psychological justification for an educational experience that maximized opportunities for the free expression of the child. But just as the child-centered phase of the earlier progressive movement broadened its ideological base by incorporating those elements of Rousseau's thinking that reflected the American liberal's commitment to freedom and equality, the alternative-free school movement of the 1960s fused A. S. Neill's Freudian-based pedagogy with the "return to nature" philosophy of Rousseau.

In *Emile*, Rousseau wrote: "Nature wants children to be children before they are men. . . . Childhood has ways of seeing, thinking, and feeling peculiar to itself; nothing can be more foolish than to substitute our ways for them."[17] Rousseau was simply reproducing in secular metaphors the early Christian message that "except ye be converted, and become as children, ye shall not enter into the kingdom of heaven." The social world of traditional customs and knowledge was to yield to the innocence and natural goodness of the unsocialized (uncorrupted) child; or to put it in terms that restore a root metaphor in both theological and secular strains of Western thought, the redemption of fallen man would be followed by a new beginning. The advocates of "free" schools were not interested in exploring the cultural roots of this theme, nor were they interested in making explicit the connections between modernization and the ready-made ideological framework that enabled them to translate the celebration of the spontaniety and innate goodness of child's actions into classroom practice. Freedom and equality were not conditional terms, but were seen as absolute guides that guaranteed that the child's expression would not be inhibited by the authority of tradition or the teacher's role. Freedom, a traditional political metaphor, became fused with the romantic idea of spontaneous experience as the highest expression of goodness. Equality, the other pillar of liberal thought, was to serve as the guideline not only for determining the bases of social relations in the classroom but also as a means of flattening the sense of time in a manner that made the immediate experience of the child the ultimate concern.

Just as Dewey served as a friendly critic of the earlier child-centered phase of progressive education, the alternative-free school movement of the 1960s had its friendly critics. But critics like Allen Graubard and Jonathan Kozol, both of whom warned against the anti-intellectualism and the naive understanding of the relationship between free schools and structural characteristics of the larger society, did not see the connection between the neoromanticism of the alternative-free schools and the crises of modernization. Their criticisms were directed toward deflating the notion that educational reform along the lines of the free schools would lead, by some kind of magic, to basic reform in American society. For them the problem was systemic, and was basically beyond the realm of what could be affected by public school reform. Ultimately, they saw the need to relate educational reform to the larger problem of social reform, particularly economic reform. It was not the vision of a nonrepressive society but the strategy of the neoromantics that was being challenged.

Although alternative-free schools do not fit into a single mold, the commonly shared ideology that highlighted the importance of freedom, equality, and the natural goodness of the child's experience served to connect the schools to the process of modernization in a way that has not generally been recognized. It was almost as though critic and friend alike were content to accept the ideology at face value. The emphasis that alternative-free schools placed on the student's immediate experience as the source of all knowledge and moral guidance canceled all other forms of traditional knowledge. Learning from an apprenticeship with a master craftsman or artist, as well as the mentor relationship, were displaced by the extreme ego-centeredness of the new ideology. Students' choices were viewed as inherently sound; thus choices leading to change were beyond any form of judgment based on external, more culturally grounded criteria. In effect, the student, through whim or rational calculation, was seen as having the power to relativize all conventions of society as long as a certain degree of respect for the rights of others was not violated. This qualification on free expression created a sense of ambiguity and the need for a balancing act that was difficult to maintain in classrooms where free expression was made the ultimate virtue. It reflected more the liberal view that free expression should conform to rules that will ensure that the social game is not overturned, rather than Durkheim's concern with the socially integrative function of moral rules.

The relativizing tendencies of modernizing mode of thought was further strengthened by the view that no body of knowledge possessed inherent authority or could be judged more worthy than any other body of knowledge. Before the tribunal of the autonomous student, all forms of knowledge and artistic expression existed at the same level of banality until the student's choice invested it with significance. Politically and existentially, ignorance of the collective memory, which comes from sharing in the accumulated knowledge of past generations, threatened the individual with what Hannah Arendt referred to as "losing the dimension of depth in human existence."[18] Culturally, the shift of authority from tradition, social mores, religious beliefs, or other sources of ultimate grounding to the individual strengthens the corrosive power of nihilism on the authority of culture. Nihilism, a concept introduced in the nineteenth century, was explained by the Russian writer, Ivan Turgenev, in terms that not only reflect the dominant ethos of Enlightenment tradition but also the ethos of the alternative-free classroom of the 1960s. In *Fathers and Sons*, young Arkody described his friend Bazarov as a "nihilist" because he was like "a man who does not bow down before any authority, who does not take any principle on faith, whatever reverence that principle is enshrined in."[19] The difference, however, between the Enlightenment view of authority and the view promoted in many alternative-free classrooms is that the former grounded authority in the rational process (which Nietzsche still saw as contributing to nihilism), while to the followers of Rousseau, authority was grounded entirely in the subjectivity of the student.

Many neoromantic educators focused attention on a different set of values that appeared more humane and pedagogically sound than the harsh authoritarianism they associated with many public schools. Basing learning on the interest of the student, and creating an environment where students had to learn to make their own decisions, appeared more appropriate in educating people to live in a democratic society. Neoromantic educators also saw themselves as critics of the technologically-driven, consumer-oriented society with its competitiveness, hierarchical social structures, and excessive materialism. What they did not see was that the modern culture they rejected depends on a population that is technically literate to the degree that it can decipher messages directing them to what should be consumed, but lacking the historical knowledge that would give them the perspective necessary for critical judgment. Ironically, the ethos required to sustain the cult of consumerism can be seen in the ego-centered, free expression, impulse release, "everything is relative" atmosphere that characterized many alternative-free classrooms. Unwittingly, neoromantics educational reformers, with their back-to-nature orientation, were contributing to relativizing those areas of culture that might have served as points of resistance to the growing imperialism of a technological social order. If we can see beyond the higher values invoked by the neoromantics, we might recognize the parallel between the support of the Italian fascist government of progressive elementary schools, which emphasized character formation and spontaneous self-expression, and the supportive alignment that exists between the form of education acquired in alternative-free schools and the authoritarianism of the techno-consumer culture.

It is painful to consider the possible connections between the values of the neoromantics and authoritarianism, but in order to put the "unthinkable" more clearly in focus it would be useful to quote an Italian critic.

> Fascism is just activity for activity's sake, the negation of any standard of truth beyond the capacity of being and doing all that one succeeds in being and doing at any moment. It is the synthesis of immediacy, of passing impulse, of uncriticized and uncritical self assertion considered as synonymous with unlimited freedom.[20]

It is not that alternative-free schools promote authoritarianism; it is more a question whether the values of freedom, equality, and individual centeredness, when made the starting point of the educational process, are allowed to overpower curricular and pedagogical practices that develop the intellectual discipline necessary for resisting authoritarianism in its more modern forms. This question is certainly part of the general discussion of the relativizing influence of the alternative-free school ideology, but it raises the much larger issue of how new forms of authoritarianism, whether a new state religion, a state bureaucracy, or hard-sell consumerism, are dependent on relativizing the traditional sources of authority. In order to pick up the line of thought connecting the main educational reform ideologies to the process of modernization it will be necessary to leave this issue in its embryonic form, with the hope that others will see the importance of examining it more fully.

The relationship between the process of relativizing the authority of traditional culture and the writings of neo-Marxist educational critics is instructive of how a vision and excessive reliance on a theoretical formula can prevent one from seeing clearly the trajectory of a modernizing culture. While they have had practically no influence on American public education, it is nevertheless important to examine briefly the views of the neo-Marxist educational critics. They possess a powerful moral vision of transforming a class-structured and exploitive society into a genuine community of humane values and social relationships; and even if the neo-Marxists recede again into relative obscurity (as they did in the 1930s), it is likely that the vision and the power (though not necessarily the truthfulness) of their theoretical framework will attract energetic adherents in the future. Like the recurrent appeal of neoromanticism in educational thought, Marxism will remain an intellectual position that will continue to attract social visionaries who cannot accept the liberal-technocrats' world of the "real is rational."

A major contribution to our understanding of public education jn the United States has been made by neo-Marxists like Samuel Bowles, Herbert Gintis, Michael Apple, and, more recently, Henry Giroux. Similar work by neo-Marxists in Canada, Great Britain, and Australia has added to a growing corpus of literature that examines the relationship between the content and organization of school knowledge and the reproduction of class divisions in society. This line of analysis, which has included significant debates between Marxists on how far to push the explanatory power of economic determinism, has brought into serious question the liberal view of schools as a meritocratic system. It has also dispelled illusions that educators might have held about the ability of schools to serve equally the interests of all segments of the community. Public schools are organized on the basis of tacit understandings about what constitutes cultural capital; students who possess the requisite amounts of cultural capital (elaborated symbolic worlds that contain both a value orientation and complex language codes) are thus processed and certified differently from students who come from homes that do not provide a rich and complex symbolic environment.

Neo-Marxist educators have extended the analysis into the complex interrelationship of class background, schooling, and work possibilities, as well as into the more esoteric questions of what constitutes hegemonic culture. But what is of interest here is the connection between their prescriptions for educational and social reform and the values that appear to be accelerating the process of cultural change. In effect, the basic question pertains to why neo-Marxist educational theorists have taken most elements of the cultural modernization for granted. This intellectual bias has resulted in the nearly total failure of neo-Marxist educators to consider the claims that history makes on us, including the continuities that *ought* to be maintained.

A partial explanation relates to the basic assumptions Marxism derived from the Englightenment. The belief that rational thought or theory is the chief means not only of grasping the nature of reality but also for directing the course of change is fundamental to the neo-Marxist educators' modernizing orientation. Paulo Freire, the Brazilian Marxist theorist of a liberation pedagogy, identifies rational thought as the essential characteristic of human nature and sees it as the means of giving humankind control over the future. As the epistemic assumptions that characterize most neo-Marxist educational theorists are stated so clearly by Freire, it would be useful to quote him at length.

> In the revolutionary perspective, the learners are invited to think. Being conscious, in this sense, is not simply a formula or a slogan. It is a radical form of being, of being human. It pertains to beings that not only know, but know that they know. The knowledge of earlier knowledge, gained by the learners as a result of analyzing praxis in its social context, opens to them the possibility of new knowledge. The new knowledge, going far beyond the limits of the earlier knowledge, reveals the reasons for being behind the facts, thus demythologizing the false interpretations of these same facts. And so, there is no more separation between thought-language and objective reality.[21]

This statement, which reflects the secular-anthropocentric universe of the Englightenment, unequivocally asserts the power of reason to grasp the nature of reality and to take control of it from the mystifying forces of history. This heroic stance appears naive when we consider how reason itself is shaped by the unconscious history embedded in the language through which we derive the cognitive maps that serve as the basis of the rational process, but it nevertheless provides an important clue to the deep antipathy that Marxist educational theorists feel toward the past.

The irony of neo-Marxist educational theorists is that they have substituted for the traditional myths a new set of myths, but they do not recognize the mythic elements that have become fused with the idea of modernization. At the center of the new mythology, which they share with both the neoromantic educators and the liberal-technocratic educators, is the belief that change is progressive. This myth (or aspect of their culturally conditioned lens) causes them to see revolutionary action and "resistance" as leading to progressive forms of social change. For example, Henry Giroux suggests that the concept of the dialectic informs how curriculum theory and practice are to be viewed. The dialectic, he writes, "incorporates an historical sensibility in the interest of liberating human beings not only from those traditions that legitimate oppressive institutional arrangements, but also from their own individual history, i.e., that which society has made of them."[22] This statement is typical of the Marxist belief, which is also shared by the bourgeois culture they wish to overturn, that time can be brought under rational control. Although this is true in a limited technological sense, it is continuously disproven in terms of human morality and in terms of the entropy of the energy base on which modern cultures are built. Why Marxists (and capitalists) have a fundamentally incorrect view of time is not the issue we want to develop here. Rather, it is the neo-Marxists' particular obsession with time that is important to understanding how their epistemic categories make them carriers of the modernizing and relativizing mode of consciousness rather than effective critics. As one observer noted, Marx himself used the *Manifesto* to celebrate the achievements of bourgeois culture and ingenuity in accelerating social change; he parted with them primarily because he saw the system of private property stalling the further development of the forces of production.[23] In more contemporary terms, Samuel Bowles and Herbert Gintis argued that "the power, class, and institutional arrangements of capitalist society do not permit the full exploitation of the benefits of those productive forces that the capitalist growth process has brought into being. . . . Capitalism is an irrational system, standing in the way of further social progress."[24] Socialism, according to Bowles and Gintis, would provide the rational basis for accelerating the rate of social progress.

While there are substantive differences between neo-Marxists, alternative-free school advocates, and liberal-technocratic educational reformers, they nevertheless share basic assumptions about the progressive nature of change and (at least in their writings on the liberating potential of education) a view of the individual as essentially good and capable of self-realization. The liberal-technocrats tend to view the individual as shaped by the environment, whereas some neo-Marxist educators hold, contrary to the determinist view of the individual that a structuralist analysis suggests, a view of the individual as capable of social agency. Paulo Freire is the best example, but the writings of other neo-Marxist educators, such as Apple and Giroux, suggest a similar orientation toward the emancipation of the individual. As these core beliefs are also basic to the modernizing mode of consciousness, these educational reformers and critics have formulated theories of education that strengthen the relativizing tendencies of modern culture. Their theories of education, while different in many respects, lead to conditioning students to expect change, to view self-realization and expression as the highest form of humanity, to adopt an anthropocentric view of the universe, and to hold a rationalized, social engineering attitude toward existential and social problems (the alternative-free school advocates would depart company with the others on this latter issue). What their theories of education do not take into account is the fact that we are not "individuals" in the way represented by our ideological folklore. The metaphors of "self-realization," "self-expression," "self-determination," which are used by all three groups to express different social claims that they want to make on behalf of individual freedom, carry certain tacit assumptions about a self-formed, self-contained, volitional being.[25] Given this view of the individual, it become logical to regard traditional mores, responsibility to a larger social entity, and historically-grounded knowledge as sources of oppression and self-alienation. Consequently, their theories of education tend to treat a knowledge of one's own history as having either instrumental significance only (the technocrat view) or as an object of demystification (the neo-Marxist view).

The ideological recipe that pictures the individual as the author of authentic choice also leads to thinking about curriculum in terms that will indulge the interest of the learner. This usually translates into offering a variety of courses that have a contemporary appeal—an educational translation of the "consumer is always right" ethic. This approach to education hides the true form of authoritarianism in a consumer-oriented culture and at the same time ensures that the student will not acquire a form of education that would demystify the liberal myth of atomistic indivudualism. A more systematic examination of one's cultural traditions might reveal that the characteristics of "individual" thought and expression reproduce the patterns of thought rooted in the past. Awareness of the past, as a prerequisite for making judgments about the cultural continuities to be maintained and sources of unconscious control, is simply not part of the conceptual framework of these educational critics. Consequently, the theories of education that characterize the technicist, neoromantic, and neo-Marxist educators fail to provide the perspective that would enable the individual to think about the direction in which their culture is developing. In effect, the student whose education is influenced by these ideological perspectives is being indoctrinated with the value orientations and assumptions that underlie a modernizing culture. It is little wonder that students feel little curiosity or concern about the problems of modernization. It is simply part of their taken-for-granted attitudes, and when social problems arise that cannot be resolved through social engineering, counselling, or chemistry, the tendency is to call for more individual freedom and social change.

For the reader who objects to the claim that neo-Marxist educators share essentially the same conventional neoromantic view of the individual's capacity for self-direction in the educational process, and thus are subject to the same criticism that is being directed at the neoromantic and technological humanists, it is instructive to read the criticisms that are being made by people who call themselves "classical Marxists." David Reynolds and Michael Sullivan, commenting on what they saw as the "recent debasement" of the radical perspective, argued that educational prescriptions that promote the "individual learner's freedom to define his own goals" were incompatible with a system of "*collectively*" defined educational goals they saw as consistent with Marxist revolutionary principles. Freedom of individual development could occur only within the context of a genuine communist society (and only after it had been achieved). But the realization of this form of society could be attained only as Marxists built on the "curricular content and pedagogy. . . . that is presently associated with the educational processes of capitalistic schooling."[26] In effect, they were suggesting that a Durkheimian rather than Rousseauistic view of individualism would provide the more correct guide for translating Marxist theory into educational practice.

SUMMARY OF THEMES

Before traditional beliefs and norms of behavior were relativized by critical rationalism, technological innovation, and the value framework that placed a premium on individual self-expression, equality, and freedom, authority existed outside the individual. In effect, the freedom of the individual (assuming the individual experienced the sense of personal agency) was restrained by a sense of authority grounded either in tradition, God, elders of the family and community, or the moral force of shared norms. As Hannah Arendt pointed out, even though authority demanded obedience, it precluded the use of external means of coercion.[27] Traditional forms of authority were an integral part of the belief system, internalized as part of the individual's cultural map, that gave structure and meaning to the life world. Authority thus operated as part of the individual's taken-for-granted attitudes. The relativizing of cultural traditions, which altered the individual's natural attitude toward authority, involved a shift whereby authority became increasingly centered in the individual.

The breakdown of a unified belief system in a society where each person assumes, as a hallmark of self-realization, the authority to define what is real and what is to be valued leads to politicizing areas of cultural belief that once were beyond the boundary of what was considered subject to negotiation. As the traditional forms of authority that Arendt identified are eroded, there is a need for negotiating a new basis of understanding and authority. In effect, this involves a political process whereby power is increasingly exercised by individuals or social groups who are able to use the communication process to substitute their definition for what previously was legitimated by traditional forms of authority. To put it another way, the relativizing of cultural traditions means that individuals and groups with greater skill in using (and manipulating) the language system will exercise power in naming and thus controlling how others will view social reality. A consequence of the process of modernization is the increased political significance that language has assumed in regulating the norms of everyday life. George Orwell helped us recognize how language is used in modern forms of authoritarian societies to manipulate the individual. In order to counter this trend, a society that values individual freedom and equality (the very value orientation that has problematized authority) must ensure that each individual be educated to exercise communicative competence. But in order to exercise communicative competence the individual must possess a knowledge of the culture that is being renegotiated. Without knowledge that is explicit and rationally based, the individual will lack, in very simple terms, the ability to enter into the negotiation process that goes on as members of society attempt to redefine those elements of the shared cultural maps that have, for one reason or another, lost their plausibility. Providing the conceptual foundations that make communicative competence possible is a challenge that faces educators. What follows is an attempt to show how the sociology of knowledge provides a theoretical framework that illuminates how the educational process can contribute to the student's communicative competence.

NOTES

1. C. A. Bowers, *Cultural Literacy for Freedom* (Eugene, Oreg.: Elan Publishers, 1974).
2. Hannah Arendt, *Between Past and Future* (Cleveland: Meridan Books, 1961), 92–93.
3. Edward Hall, *Beyond Culture* (Garden City, N.Y.: Anchor Books, 1977), 44.
4. Arnold van Gennep, *The Rites of Passage* (Chicago: The University of Chicago Press, 1975), 21.
5. Robert Bellah, *Beyond Belief: Essays on Religion in a Post Traditional World* (New York: Harper & Row, 1970), 67.
6. Alvin Gouldner, *The Future of the Intellectual and the Rise of a New Class* (New York: Seabury Press, 1979), 28–31.
7. Arnold Gehlen, *Man in the Age of Technology* (New York: Columbia University Press, 1980), 102.
8. Daniel Bell, "Beyond Modernism, Beyond Self," in *Art, Politics, and Will*, ed. Quentin Anderson, Stephen Donadio, and Steven Marcus (New York: Basic Books, 1977), 219.
9. For a useful discussion of how we remain in the grip of tradition, see Edward Shils, *Tradition* (Chicago: University of Chicago Press, 1981).
10. Lucian Goldmann, *The Philosophy of the Enlightenment: The Christian Burgess, and the Enlightenment* (Cambridge, Mass.: MIT Press, 1968), 54.
11. Daniel Bell, *The Winding Passage* (New York: Basic Books, 1980), 333.
12. See, "The Return of the Sacred: The Argument on the Future of Religion" in Bell, *The Winding Passage*, 324–352. Also see Thomas Luckmann, *The Invisible Religion* (London: Macmillan, 1967).
13. Irving Howe, ed., *The Idea of the Modern in Literature and the Arts* (New York: Horizon Press, 1967), 13.
14. Ibid., 19.
15. For a highly useful analysis of the emerging ideology that justifies the role of intellectuals and experts, see Ben Knights, *The Idea of the Clerisy in the Nineteenth Century* (Cambridge, England: Cambridge University Press, 1978). Also see the writings of Comte and Marx; both writers saw reason as a progressive force that freed mankind from commonsense forms of knowledge (i.e., superstition, myth, folk knowledge, and prejudice).

16. Peter L. Berger and Hansfried Kellner, *Sociology Reinterpreted: An Essay on Method and Vocation* (Garden City, N.Y.: Anchor Books, 1981), 154.
17. Author unknown, *Writing Behavioral Objectives*, (Issued by the school district office to the teachers of Eugene, Oregon), 4,6. Italics added.
18. Hannah Arendt, *Between Past and Future*, 94.
19. Ivan Turgenev, *Fathers and Sons*, trans. Rosemary Edmonds (Harmondsworth, England: Penguin Books, 1975), 94.
20. From the fascinating and valuable study by Harold Entwistle, *Antonio Gramsci: Conservative Schooling for Radical Politics* (London: Routledge and Kegan Paul, 1979), 86. For a useful discussion of Giovanni Gentile's view of the pupil as the "living center of the school," see H. S. Harris, *The Social Philosophy of Giovanni Gentile* (Urbana: University of Illinois Press, 1960). Gentile was Mussolini's minister of education and oversaw the reform of the Italian educational system.
21. Paulo Freire, *Pedagogy in Process: The Letters to Guinea-Bissau* (New York: Seabury Press, 1978), 24.
22. Henry A. Giroux, *Ideology, Culture and the Process of Schooling* (Philadelphia: Temple University Press, 1981), 118.
23. Alvin W. Gouldner, *The Two Marxisms: Contradictions and Anomolies in the Development of Theory* (New York: Seabury Press, 1980), 384.
24. Samuel Bowles and Herbert Gintis, *Schooling in Capatalistic America* (New York: Basic Books, 1976), 275.
25. An interesting contrast to the educational theorist's commitment to the idea of individualism is contained in William M. Sullivan, *Reconstructing Public Philosophy* (Berkeley: University of California Press, 1982). See also Fred R. Dallmayr, *Twilight of Subjectivity: Contributions to a Post-Individualistic Theory of Politics* (Amherst: The University of Massachusetts Press, 1981).
26. David Reynolds and Michael Sullivan, "Towards a New Socialist Sociology of Education," in *Schooling Ideology and the Curriculum*, ed. Len Barton, Roland Meighan, and Stephan Walker (Barcombe, Lewes: Falmer Press, 1980), 184
27. Arendt, *Between Past and Future*, 93.

2

Theoretical Foundations of Communicative Competence

In the most fundamental sense, formal education is a process of communication. Communication, as an essential aspect of socialization, is the medium through which we acquire our conceptual maps that enable us to operate in everyday society; it also sustains our sense of reality against the erosion of prolonged silence. To put it in a manner similar to Dewey's formulation, education, communication, and socialization are nearly interchangeable terms. In that education always involves communication, and therefore socialization, we must acknowledge the dual nature of socialization as having the potential to liberate thought and facilitate the communication of new ideas to others; it is also a binding force that may prevent people from seeing how their lives are shaped by social conventions. Viewed in terms of the life of a single individual, socialization may lead to emancipated ways of thinking about certain areas of existence while sustaining traditional beliefs and practices in other areas. The person who is creative as an artist or social theorist may be quite conventional in other ways. In fact, the areas of existence made nonproblematic by the power of socialization to reproduce traditional values and patterns of behavior may make it possible for the individual to focus the attention and energy necessary to be more original in terms of other facets of life. Because of this dual potential, it is impossible to make a sweeping generalization about socialization, just as it is impossible to make sweeping generalizations about education. Both have the potential to liberate and bind, consequently both are continually problematic in an existential sense. Even the liberating and binding processes are problematic, as neither can be judged simply on its own terms as being inherently good.

The problem is to find the right balance between the potential of socialization to liberate and to bind, so that both the individual and society can grow in a manner that integrates the new with the positive aspects of the past. In recent years, the educational fellowers of both Marx and Rousseau upheld a vision of a new social order that was to be free of all forms of oppression, tradition, and, presumably, of the socialization process itself. People, so the vision held, were to fulfill the Enlightenment dream of freedom, equality and reason by becoming the author of their own existence. This vision, which is like a recurring distemper of romanticism, suggests that neither the inevitability of socialization, nor its dual nature of positive and negative effects are understood.

A theory of education that arises out of a concern with the future adequacy of the assumptions on which our culture is based and with people's ability to exercise communicative competence in reconstructing essential elements of our cultural maps, must be grounded in a careful understanding of the complexities of socialization. Unless the dynamics of socialization are taken into account, along with culture's pattern for organizing reality, educational theories are likely to be little more than expressions of well intended visions that have little chance of being realized anywhere. The visionary approach, unfortunately, only serves to undermine a more persistent, less spectacular form of reform effort by creating cycles of euphoria followed by disillusionment and general cynicism toward the prospects of any form of social change. Overlooking the nature of socialization can also result in underestimating the genuine contributions formal education can make to solving social problems.

Our central task will be to examine how socialization contributes to acquiring the conceptual maps on which daily life is based. Viewing learning in terms of socialization should also help to clarify how formal education contributes to a kind of false consciousness where individuals feel powerless to rethink their belief system because they either lack the necessary symbolic tools or have been led to believe that reality is the same as what their belief system says it is. After developing the theory of socialization and showing its relationship to the educational process I will, in the following chapters, identify those principles of learning that can serve as a guide for reforming how knowledge is organized in school curricula. In effect, our ultimate purpose will be to identify the "moves" in the language game of socialization that can lead to a more liberating form of education.

Before we begin, however, a few cautionary remarks are in order. What we shall be examining—the dynamics of how our own everyday sense of reality is constituted through interaction with others—is such an integral part of how we experience the world that we generally lack the necessary distance and objectivity to see it clearly. And when we become aware of our taken-for-granted experience, or the categories and assumptions we use as the rules for interpreting experience, there is often such a sense of familiarity, even inevitability, it is often difficult to generate much enthusiasm or concern for making the intellectual effort to examine them. Exploring the geography of our own consciousness is not nearly as exciting as announcing the end of social classes or that schools are oppressive institutions that destroy the freedom and natural goodness of the child. But it is more important if we are to begin the process of reconstituting the basic way we organize and experience our cultural reality. The possibility of cultural literacy that leads to communicative competence involves many variables and is so problematic in an existential sense that it cannot, in good faith, be announced with any sense of messianic fervor. Even though the results will be incremental and appear glacially slow when judged against the dimensions of the cultural crisis that is being brought on by the growth in the world's population and the decrease in natural resources, it is the only option open to us. Revolutionary change that simply accelerates the very processes of modernization that have led to the ecological crisis and the erosion the cultural inheritance, cannot be considered as a viable alternative, even though it seems to provide a sense of romantic adventure that is increasingly difficult to experience in the impersonal world of a technocracy.

At a general level of understanding, socialization is seen as the process of learning the habits, norms, and ways of thinking essential for fitting into society. This view, which is widely held among the general populace, emphasizes the adaptive nature of socialization; according to this view successful socialization becomes, in effect, successful social adjustment. While this formulation has the virtue of simplicity and appears to provide a necessary criterion for distinguishing nondeviant from deviant behavior, it nevertheless is totally inadequate as an explanatory theory. This simplistic formulation is retained for other reasons, namely it serves as part of an ideology that can be invoked to justify interventions intended to adapt people's behavior to prevailing bureaucratic and social norms. But this view of socialization is too general and value-oriented to serve as a theory of learning for the more thoughtful teachers. What I hope to do here is to identify basic elements of the socialization that are obscured by viewing it as a process of social adjustment, and to show how this more complex view of socialization can be used as a general theory of learning for guiding educational change.

From infancy through adulthood, socialization occurs continuously and one could almost say effortlessly, if it were not for the occasional situation where disapproval and punishment are a result of an unwillingness or inability to learn what is socially expected. The small child learns through the normal everyday process of interacting with others a wide and complex range of cultural knowledge that serves as the recipes for conducting everyday life. The child also learns how to operate in terms of the language systems that govern the use of time, space (both public and private) and technology. Children learn, for example, the typified sense of time that enables them to experience it as a linear phenomenon and to make the appropriate distinctions between when time is being wasted, saved, or properly spent. In terms of the language of space, they learn how others perceive the use of different kinds of social space (e.g., how to vary the communication process as they move from intimate, personal relationships within the family to the more distant impersonal relationships of the street and market place). As the range of contact with the social world increases their stock of recipe knowledge of everyday reality increases along with their skill in exhibiting the socially sanctioned responses. As the individual moves through adolescence to adulthood the process of socialization continues, expanding the set of interpretational rules in proportion to the new social settings that are successfully encountered.

The point here is not to provide a complete survey of the learning, a geography of social consciousness, that occurs through socialization, but to suggest something of its range, complexity, and the naturalness of its occurance. I also want to suggest that it be viewed as a process of learning that is so effective (some might say too effective) that the individual is often unaware of what is being learned. In stressing that socialization is a process of learning, and that the process of socialization continues as the basic (perhaps only) form of learning that occurs in school settings, we can see more clearly the need to understand how the dynamics of socialization relate to the educational reform efforts being proposed here. In order to focus the analysis I will use an example of socialization in a school setting and then proceed to identify the process of socialization in terms of a series of propositions. This analysis will help to put in focus important concepts in the sociology of knowledge developed by Alfred Schutz, Peter Berger, and Thomas Luckmann, that will be used later for suggesting reforms in school curricula and in the role of the teacher.

The example, which could be taken from numerous educational settings, has the essential characteristics of taken for grantedness that we want to explore.

> The observer is just entering the fifth-grade classroom for the observation period. The teacher says, "which one of you nice, polite boys would like to take (the observer's) coat and hang it up?" From the waving hands, it would seem that all would like to claim the title. The teacher chooses one child, who takes the observer's coat. The teacher says, "Now, children, who will tell (the observer) what we have been doing?"
>
> The usual forest of hands appears, and a girl is chosen to tell. . . . The teacher conducted the arithmetic lessons mostly by asking, "who would like to tell the answers to the next problem?" This question was usually followed by the apparently much competition to answer.[1]

The following proposition derived from the theories of Schutz, Berger, and Luckmann help to explain how the values and beliefs of our culture are communicated and internalized into consciousness as part of the student's conceptual map.

PROPOSITION 1. *Social reality is shared, sustained and continuously negotiated through communication.*

As Peter Berger put it, "The reality of the world is sustained through conversation with significant others."[2] Returning to the example, the sense of nice boys competing with each other to hang up the observer's coat is sustained through the dialectic of teacher-student communication. Drawing upon her own conceptual map the teacher typified the meaning of "nice, polite boys" by giving the clue of how nice boys were to act. The students help to sustain the teacher's definitions of the situation with verbal and body language that conforms to the teacher's expectation. The interaction between teacher and students is an example of how fragile the sense of meaning is in social settings, and how, through conversation, the nuances of meaning and mutual expectations are negotiated (the word "negotiation" is not being used here to mean a confrontation between individuals of equal power). If the students had ignored the teacher's request or confronted her in a hostile manner her sense of expectancy would probably have been transformed into a sense of disappointment or anger, and a sense of concern about how to discipline boys who were not acting "nice" when there is a guest in the room. As Berger says, "In a very fundamental sense it can be said that one converses one's way through life."[3]

In addition to sustaining the shared definitions of situations and serving as the medium for negotiating different understandings, communication also provides the primary means of sharing the knowledge of everyday life with new members. Geoffrey Esland was referring to the reality sharing and constituting function of communication when he observed that "through language culture becomes existential: that is, it becomes part of the identities and self-conceptions of members of society, and forms the basis for their reasoning and reflection."[4] Through verbal and body language communicated by others, individuals acquire the interpretational rules and assumptions of the culture that enables them to experience reality in a manner that is congruent with the reality experienced by others. Thus communication is not only essential to sustaining the agreed upon conventions of belief and action, but in initiating new members into the socially shared knowledge. To put it another way, through the process of communication, social reality is being continuously renewed in the consciousness of new members, while at the same time undergoing a process of gradual revision as each participant negotiates minor changes (and occasionally major ones) that reflect differences in perspective and existential stance. The objective sense of social reality as we know it—the roles we play, the institutions that dictate our behavior, and the conventions that influence how time, competition and authority shape our experience—exists in consciousness and is sustained through communication. (The dynamics of this process will be explored later.) John Dewey summed this up when he said that society exists in communication and then identified learning with communication. George H. Mead, who greatly influenced the stream of the sociology of knowledge we are using here, similarly identified communication as both essential to the formation of self consciousness and to sustaining the traditions and membership in a social group.

PROPOSITION II. *Through socialization the individual's intersubjective self is built up in a biographically unique way, and it serves as the set of interpretational rules for making sense of everyday life.*

The concept of the intersubjective is a means of accounting for how culture (the socially shared stock of knowledge, including language) becomes internalized into the individual's consciousness and experienced as the natural order of things. Cognitive psychologists explain the internalizing of other people's cultural maps in terms of a "schemata" the individual uses to interpret experience, recall information, and to imagine future possibilities.[5] The intersubjective accounts for how the experience of significant others become part of one's own life world. It also is essential to explaining how one individual can understand the experience of another person. The intersubjective is, in effect, the socially derived set of assumptions, definitions, typifications and recipe knowledge that serves as the individual's frame of reference that underlies perception, cognition and behavior. It functions like a cultural lense that causes the individual to experience social reality according to the underlying grammar (rules) of the culture.

In terms of the example of students competing to hang up the visitor's coat, the prior socialization of all participants—teacher, students, and observer—involved internalizing into their respective frames of reference (intersubjective self) a common set of understandings, definitions, and assumptions that functioned as a code, causing the behaviors of the participants to evolve in a predictable manner. The teacher's intersubjective self (built up through past socialization) included taken-for-granted definitions and assumptions (e.g., the cultural rules for receiving a guest in the classroom; the assumption about how nice boys act and that boys, rather than girls, hang up the guest's coat; the idea that motivation can be stimulated and controlled by activating competitiveness among the students ["Which one of you would like to take the observer's coat?"], and the realization that students obtain the teacher's attention by raising their hand). The student's intersubjective self was socially programmed with the same set of definitions and assumptions—raising hands, competing for the teacher's attention, wanting to fit the teacher's tacit definition of a "nice boy." The communication that served as the medium for the unfolding of the culturally prefigured social drama simply served to reinforce the correctness and naturalness of the rules each of the participants were using to interpret their role in the drama. The inter-subjective served as the mental template that guided each person and enabled all of the participants to anticipate the probable response of the others. Yet the participants, as we can observe in our own experience, were undoubtedly unaware of the system of cultural controls. As Edward Hall points out, awareness of the code that governs experience in different social settings operates according to the principle of negative feedback: one becomes aware of the control system only when the hidden program is not followed.[6]

The intersubjective self is cumulatively built up as the individual internalizes the definitions, assumptions and typifications communicated by significant others. Language acquisition plays a crucial role in consti-tuting the individual's intersubjective self because language is a primary carrier of the socially shared typifications and categories which serve as the symbol systems or codes we use to give meaning to experience. The range of culture encoded in language and acquired by the individual becomes a powerful determinant of what the individual will be able to think and communicate. This is why the arrested or constrained commu-nication that characterizes certain areas of the curriculum becomes such an important factor in the student's socialization. In effect, the school's power to legitimatize and restrict how cultural experience is symbolized through language becomes an important factor in the development of the student's schemata or intersubjective self (or frame of reference governing the interpretation of everyday life).

Before going on to the next proposition, several points need to be made about the implications of the intersubjective self in terms of how we think about objectivity, behaviorism, and individualism. The theory of the intersubjective self, in effect, challenges in the most fundamental manner the ideas of objective knowledge, behavior shaped by the contin-gencies of the environment, and atomistic individuals who assert their total freedom from "social oppression." The idea of objective knowledge carries with it certain assumptions that dichotomizes the subject (the knower) from the object (the known). This radical separation, which is essential to the notion of objectivity, cannot exist except as a social convention, if we acknowledge how the external social world is internal-ized into the knower's frame of reference in the form of a cultural grammar that influences what will be seen, the categories that will be used to interpret the phenomena, and the language of communication. In effect, the intersubjective part of conscious awareness participates in constituting the known world according to a symbol system that is derived from the culture; the individual does not "discover" an independently constituted reality in the passive, naive manner suggested by the empiricist.

In terms of the more extreme formulations of behaviorism, the existence of the intersubjective self helps us to recognize how our cultural maps influence what we are conscious of, and how behavior follows from the conscious processes of interpreting, giving meaning, and imagining possibilities. The followers of B. F. Skinner, in accepting the claims of positivism about objective knowledge, tend to ignore the meaning constituting the nature of consciousness because they lack the theoretical means of reconciling a dialective view of human consciousness with the epistemological reductionism of positivism. They resolve the problem by denying the existence of a problem: for them, behavior is the primary reality, and any changes in behavior are to be explained by the contingencies of reinforcement in the environment. If they were to incorporate the intersubjective into behaviorist theory, their position would undergo such a profound transformation that the term "behaviorism" would no longer serve as an adequate label.

The last position I want to examine briefly before ending this digression relates to the view of radical individualism. The neoromantics of the alternative school movement attempted to organize the educational experience in accordance with the idea of an autonomous individual who makes free choices. The neo-Marxists seemed to be making a similar assumption when they upheld the vision of the individual free of social oppression. What separates the two visions is that the neoromantic saw the child achieving the state of freedom as adults relinquish their authoritarian role; the neo-Marxists saw the problem of the oppressed individual rooted in the class structure. What neither position takes into account is the adequacy of the Enlightenment idea of the free individual, an idea revitalized in recent years by some existential writers. The concept of the intersubjective self, which takes account of language as a carrier of the culture's deep assumptions and categories and the function of language in providing the interpretational rules for making sense and communicating about daily experience, becomes an irrefutable basis for arguing that there is no such thing as the autonomous individual (as the neoromantic educators claim) or the individual free of oppression (as the neo-Marxist educators promise). The internalization into individual consciousness of the symbols and rules which govern cognitive functions indicates that "free" choices reflect what individuals are able to imagine in terms of their intersubjective self. Similarly, if people have a language that enables them to interact symbolically with their environment their consciousness has been "oppressed," to use the metaphor of the neo-Marxist educators. Using a different term, we could say that the individual's consciousness is encoded through the acquired language with the culture's "schemes of perception, its exchanges, its techniques, its values, the hierarchy of its practices."[7] In other words, it is the world in which the individual feels at home. What these two groups of well-intentioned reformers overlook is that socialization *always* involves the acquisition of the culture's code for organizing reality, and without a cultural code of some kind, the individual would not be able to think or communicate. The cultural code internalized into the intersubjective both facilitates conscious awareness and constrains it within definite boundaries. The real problem is not the oppression-freedom dichotomy of those who hold the Enlightenment vision of autonomous individual, but a more complex one that involves a process of making explicit the message system thus enabling them to reconstitute those aspects of the intersubjective reality (frame of reference or cultural code) that limits our ability to see and cope with important psychological, social and ecological problems.

PROPOSITION III. *Much of the social world of everyday life is learned and experienced by the individual as the natural, even inevitable order of reality. This natural attitude toward the everyday world is experienced as taken for granted.*

Returning to our example of the classroom, we can see how the teacher used the process of communication to signal to students the behavior that should be exhibited when a guest enters the room. The teacher was simply sharing with the students, while prompting them to follow the cues, her taken-for-granted sense of how to greet a guest and how to put the student's performance on display. Her natural attitude toward the situation became the scenario students were expected to incorporate into the intersubjective self as the natural attitude. Undoubtedly, the guest had also been socialized to a similar set of behavior expectations which would further reinforce the teacher's taken for granted feelings toward the social ritual that unfolded. The students were involved as learner-participants acquiring through the teacher's unintended teaching the set of natural attitudes that would enable them, when adults, to conduct the same ritual as the teacher conducted.

Viewed more generally, much of what is learned through socialization is experienced by the individual as the taken-for-granted reality. Learning when to maintain eye contact, how to write from left to right, how to win without being socially offensive (or to lose without causing others to feel guilt or embarrassment), are examples of the socially shared stock of knowledge individuals acquire as part of their natural attitude. This learning occurs through symbolic interaction with significant others and is continuous as the individual moves through the different zones and spaces of social life. As individuals internalize (often making minor changes as they interpret what the other person is communicating) the taken-for-granted attitudes of others, a stock of knowledge is built up that serves as the recipes for defining and acting in different social situations.

Edward Hall referred to the recipe knowledge that governs our behavior as the "cultural unconscious."[8] The idea of the "cultural unconscious" points to the fact that socialization involves a tacit form of learning (and teaching) of many of the conventions that govern an individual's beliefs and behavior. When beliefs and social definitions are communicated as taken for granted, they are often experienced by the individual undergoing socialization as being nonproblematic, which assures that they will be likely incorporated into the individual's frame of reference at the same tacit level of awareness.

Because of the psychological and linguistic characteristics of the natural attitude, it is often difficult to become explicitly aware of how the sense of taken-for-grantedness shapes experience and limits human freedom. Ivan Illich, in arguing for deschooling, made the assumption that individuals would be able to exercise freedom in choosing what they needed to learn if formal educational institutions were disbanded. What Illich overlooked was the power of the taken-for-granted beliefs to constrain imagination, to shape interpretations along already established lines, and, in a word, to be self perpetuating. Existential writers often share Illich's naive ideas about human freedom. If the sense of taken-for-grantedness (i.e., the teacher's natural attitude toward student performance as a competitive event) prevents a person from imagining other possibilities, there is no free choice. Similarly, a person will not ask to learn about those aspects of culture which are already part of his or her taken-for-granted reality. Existential choice is not grounded in the individual's accumulated recipe knowledge, but in those areas of liminality not already stabilized and deproblematized by the natural attitude. The point that needs stressing in terms of the relation of existential freedom to the individual's natural attitude is that awareness of the binding power of one's own culture comes about through a form of reflexive thinking that at first will feel unnatural.

PROPOSITION IV. *The individual's self-concept is constituted through interaction with significant others: the individual not only acquires the socially shared knowledge but also an understanding of who she/he is in relation to it.*

As George H. Mead has pointed out, a self concept is socially acquired as the individual interacts with significant others. While it has a biological basis in the need to construct a symbolic world of meaning, the fact that it is socially acquired has important implications in terms of an individual's dependency on others. The dynamics of self-corcept formation identified by Mead essentially involve the significant other (parent, teacher, peers, etc.) in a relationship where they define through their recipe knowledge the nature of a social situation and through the dialectic of communication provide the behavioral clues and guidance the individual is to follow. If we return to our example and suppose that the class was a group of first graders who had not had a guest come to their room before, we can see more clearly the relationship between socialization where the individual is learning for the first time how to define a social situation, the behaviors appropriate to it, and the process of learning about one's identity in that situation. The significant other, the teacher, asks the boys who would like to be nice and polite and communicates how the situation is defined through the cues for how to demonstrate being nice and polite. As the boys perform in this situation the significant other communicates through verbal and body language her sense of approval and disapproval of how well the boys have understood and performed in the situation. One is selected (the ethnographer has omitted reporting the complex range of communication involved in these everyday rituals), while the other boys who did not achieve the level of performance desired by the teacher were not. The girls are simply left out of the competition to be nice and polite because at that time girls were to be passive rather than assertive and to be the recipients of male care and protection (like having doors opened for them, having their coats hung up, etc.) The students develop the concept of themselves in that situation by internalizing the teacher's response to their performance. As an African poet put it: "In your presence I know my name." At this initial stage of self-concept development, the ambiguity the student would feel about what is happening is overcome by using the teacher's responses that are communicated in the gestures of approval and disapproval as a reference point for establishing their own identity in the situation.

The individual's self concept, at this initial stage of socialization, involves internalizing the significant other's responses.[9] This reflexive act of seeing oneself through the responses of significant others overcomes the uncertainty and vulnerability that a person experiences in new social situations, but it is often achieved at the price of internalizing a concept of self that reflects the significant other's unexamined beliefs and unresolved psychological problems. This internalized self image may, on the other hand, be shaped by values that have emerged from a long process of reflection and insight. The important point to be made here is that the individual, during the initial stage of socialization to the definitions and expectations of a new social situation, is in a dependency relationship where few of the values and assumptions that form the basis of judgment are clarified or subject to any genuine negotiation process.

The normal individual's self-concept reflects the range of social interaction. As the individual has a wider range of social experiences—acting out different roles, competing and interacting with others in a variety of social settings, working with materials and expressing ideas, and the like—the definition of who one is in terms of these social activities becomes established in consciousness as the individual's self-concept. Individuals, as they grow in self-confidence and the ability to make their own commitments to values and ideas, may begin to exercise increasing control over the selection of the significant other and in the process gain considerable control over how they define themselves. But this mature, relatively invulnerable self is not achieved without effort or considerable social risk. The dynamics of the socialization process tend to foster dependence, particularly in terms of the power of the significant other to define "what is" and to legitimate the individual's performance and thus how to think about one's self-image. Dependence is also the outcome of internalizing the significant other's language code for transmitting the taken-for-granted knowledge that gives structure and continuity to social experience.

An important aspect of the individual's self-concept is its connection with the socially derived stock of knowledge that serves as the natural set of interpretational rules for organizing experience. This connection between how we know and interpret the world and the individual's personal sense of identity was recognized by Friedrich Nietzsche when he said that our interpretations of everyday life were more than simple expressions of objective knowledge and understanding since they were grounded in the deeply rooted psychological processes of identity maintenance. This connection between self-identity and the socially derived knowledge codes (e.g., expressed in the threat to self identity caused by unemployment) means that individuals have a degree of ego-investment in maintaining those definitions and assumptions upon which their self-concept is based. Abraham Maslow and others have pointed out that persons who are insecure in terms of identity tends to distort their perception in order to retain the prefigured beliefs that provide the basis of the limited psychological security they possess. The individual who has a more maturally developed self-concept, on the other hand, possesses the psychological strength to move into the zones of liminality that occur when the taken-for-granted dimensions of culture are problematized. For this individual, problematizing provides an opportunity to grow in reflexive self understanding. This relation between identity and belief system becomes a crucial factor in the socialization of students which we shall deal with more fully in the next chapter.

PROPOSITION V. *Human consciousness is characterized by intentionality; it is the intentionality of consciousness that insures that socialization is not deterministic.*

Phenomenologists have suggested that human consciousness should be understood as a verb; that is, consciousness always involves awareness of something—being conscious of the objects of movement in one's immediate surroundings, being conscious of inner feelings, being aware of the resemblance of a person to the past. In saying that consciousness (the phenomenology of awareness) has an object, it must also be emphasized that consciousness is intentional in the sense that a choice is made (awareness is directed intentionally) as to the object of consciousness. As the individual moves through social space, for example, the intentional nature of consciousness is expressed in terms of what will be chosen as the object of awareness. Consciousness is not a tabula rasa on which the outside world impresses itself, as light does on the film of a camera. Individuals can choose to be momentarily aware of the entire physical and social space in which they find themselves; they can also determine the duration of awareness as well as choose as the object of consciousness a single object such as the dress of a solitary individual. This intentional characteristic of consciousness can easily be seen if we attend to our own phenomenology of awareness. As we move through the different zones of social reality, we will find ourselves moving from floodlight consciousness to spotlight consciousness, attending to the immediate problem of avoiding a collision with another person who is not aware of where they are walking, remembering aspects of one's personal past, imagining future possibilities in terms of being with friends or having a moment of quiet, interpreting what a person meant by communicating in a certain tone of voice, and the like. The boundaries and foci of awareness constantly change, and it is the intentionality of consciousness that changes them.

While the intentionality of consciousness is free (not determined) in a fundamental sense, it is influenced, nevertheless, in varying degrees by the symbolic codes that have been internalized into intersubjective self through the process of socialization. For example, the intentionality of the observer in the classroom was influenced by the taken-for-granted attitudes that caused her to experience herself as an ethnographer rather than as a poet or fire inspector. Her intentionality was channelled by the definitions and assumptions shared by other ethnographers. But within the boundaries defined by her role she made choices about what to be aware of, the duration of awareness, and what was relevant to her task. The phenomenology of the teacher and students were similarly influenced by the roles orchestrated by the teacher. Yet within the even more constrained boundaries shaped by teacher expectation and continued evaluation, the consciousness of the students was still characterized by intentionality: the students were interpreting, giving meaning, imagining (possibly of events that would have been seen as subversive by the teacher), focusing on the specific event of the teacher's smile, and taking the whole thing in as an exciting opportunity to be noticed by a stranger.

The symbolic codes that serve as grammars for how to think and act within different social settings both free the intentional possibilities of consciousness within the culturally sanctioned zones of experience and deny it access to others not recognized by the culture. Thus the existence of intentionality should not be interpreted as an either-or possibility, but as an element of consciousness that can, in varying degrees, be determined (e.g., the incest taboo, linear sense of time, etc.) and shaped by the sense of taken-for-grantedness and typifications of everyday life. The unique social biography of people, their perspective in social and physical space, and their awareness of different interpretative schemas insure that the intentionality of consciousness is not controlled entirely by determinism. The intentionality of consciousness, it should be added, even plays an active, transcedent role in the individual's own socialization; for example, the social world that is encountered by the individual is selected, interpreted, given meaning, ignored, remembered, and imagined. Even while the individual is acquiring the social grammar that enables her or him to experience a shared reality, the individual's intentional consciousness acts as an accomplice in the negotiation of that social reality.

SOCIALIZATION: DEPENDENCY AND INEQUALITY

As pointed out earlier, the need to think and communicate makes socialization both necessary and inevitable. As socialization involves a sharing on the part of the already initiated individual with the uninitiated, it can be described as a relation in which the participants do not possess equal power in the specific setting in which socialization occurs. To state it more generally, socialization implies inequality among individuals in the most basic sense. As some educational reformers use the context-free metaphor of "equality" as a central ideal in their blueprints for the new society, it is important to emphasize within the context of our discussion of socialization that genuine equality among people, in all dimensions of the term (social, economic, political, psychological, linguistic, etc.) could be attained only in a society if socialization did not occur. Everybody would have to share either the same mute, primordial, presocialized state for being, or they would have to be born into the world with the completed symbolic codes necessary for maintaining a social world as part of their biological endowment. Since both are impossibilities (unless scientists succeed in replacing the symbolic world of culture with genetic engineering), we need to explore the inherent sources of inequality that exist at the microlevel, as one person socializes another person to think and act in a socially congruent manner. The inherent inequality can be viewed variously as a form of dependency, as a relationship involving unequal power, or as a form of sharing that enables an individual to learn the social stock of knowledge built up over generations and thus to escape the powerlessness that might be experienced if not given any conceptual tools to use and build on. As pointed out earlier, socialization both binds and liberates; this dual potential must be kept clearly in mind as we explore the dynamics of vulnerability in the socialization process in order to increase our understanding of how socialization (involving a relationship between unequal individuals) can lead to personal growth. Exploring the dynamics of vulnerability should enable us to see more clearly the dynamics that facilitate the human potential.

The inherent dependency that exists when socialization occurs is an expression of the fact that one of the participants possesses cultural capital, to use Pierre Bourdieu's phrase, that is not possessed by the individual being socialized. The cultural capital is the social stock of knowledge that the individual has acquired from interacting with others. This cultural capital consists of the symbolic knowledge (language codes, rules, assumptions, images, and conceptual models) that serves as the set of interpretational rules for operating in the everyday world. In terms of the larger picture of how cultural capital is distributed, the social class in which one is a member is a powerful determinant of who will have access to the cultural capital of society. But at the interpersonal level of socialization, which still may be influenced by class considerations, cultural capital is being shared when the parents communicates to the child their recipe knowledge for conceptualizing basic aspects of experience: to recognize and relate to authority, to react to failure, to compete, to understand the nature of time and to use it responsibly, and the like. This dependency relationship, which transcends considerations of social class and ethnic cultures, is rooted in the power of the significant other to define the nature of a social situation and the appropriate ways of thinking and acting in that situation for the individual who has not yet been initiated to that part of the social stock of knowledge. To use Alvin Gouldner's phrase, inequality is rooted in the significant other's power to define "what is."

The dynamics of vulnerability are not generally seen by either partner in the socialization process, consequently the process of binding is often carried out in the same benevolent, helping atmosphere that exists when more facilitating forms of socialization occur. Socialization's tacit characteristics result from the fact that the person who is the agent of socialization (e.g., the docent who instructs children how to act in a museum) is simply sharing with the children the socially acquired frame of reference that establishes what has meaning in that social setting. Since the definition of what being in a museum means (or how to act as a clerk or assistant professor, etc.) generally is an expression of the socializing agent's recipe knowledge, there is less possibility to problematize and renegotiate the basic definitions on which individuals predicate their actions. One should also recognize that the socializing agent generally has an identity investment in the recipe knowledge to which she or he was successfully socialized. This psychological investment in the definitions and assumptions that make up the social stock of knowledge often serves, as Berger and others have pointed out, as a defense against the disorientating experience of anomie. Consequently, when the significant other naively shares basic recipe beliefs with the uninitiated individual the significant others are often putting their own identities on the line. Questioning how the social situation is being defined can easily lead to putting the significant other's identity in doubt.

The individual being socialized not only has to deal with the politics of identity negotiation, but at the initial stages is dependent upon the language code made available by the significant other for thinking about the social experience. If the significant other is sharing with the child a taken-for-granted understanding of time, work, or responsibility, it is likely that these beliefs will be communicated through a limited vocabulary. The vocabulary and rules governing the relevant categories of thought will be limited to what is necessary to communicate efficiently the significant other's recipe knowledge. The sense of taken-for-grantedness further obscures the need to introduce a more complex language code that might problematize the situation.

Vulnerability in the socialization process is also maintained by the objectifying characteristic of language. Peter Berger and Thomas Luckmann observed that the "detachment of language lies much more basically in its capacity to communicate meanings that are not direct expressions of subjectivity 'here and now.' . . . language is capable of becoming the objective repository of vast accumulations of meaning and experience, which it can then preserve in time and transmit to following generations."[10] This capacity of language to represent meanings as objectively real and independent of the individuals who communicate them makes it difficult for the participants to recognize that meanings, values, interpretations—what becomes stabilized symbolically as objective knowledge—have a human origin. The textbook accounts of the hierarchical organization or work, the association of poverty with income level, and the treatment of technology as synonomous with progress, all present the reader with "knowledge" that appears to be objectively real and free of cultural relativity and human interpretation. Similarly, when individuals share their taken-for-granted understandings with others, this knowledge is generally communicated as objectively real. The subject-predicate structure of language mystifies the existential involvement in the communication process. Talk and the printed word often appear as objective reporting on an external state of affairs, and in the process, human authorship is difficult to establish.

As individuals undergoing socialization encounter more areas of the collective cultural experience represented as objectified reality they are likely to experience an increasing sense of existential powerlessness about what is established in consciousness as the natural order of reality. For example, women who first began to question the collective recipe knowledge that stigmatized them as intellectually and physically inferior often experienced guilt for entertaining emergent, socially unsanctioned ideas. The natural vulnerability of the socialization process, however, insures that most people's thoughts will continue to express the deep categories and assumptions embedded in the language code they naively acquired from significant others who transmitted them with equal naiveté.

As we have developed the theory, it becomes clear that socialization, sedimented as the individual's intersubjective self, influences the existential life of the individual. The acquired symbolic codes, in effect, become powerful shapers of the individual's freedom, identity and sense of ontological groundedness, and the forms of alienation that will be experienced.

Existential choice is thus expanded in proportion to the complexity of the symbolic code the individual acquires. A complex symbolic world provides the means for choosing among different interpretational schemes, as well as imagining future possibilities that would result from different scenarios (also involving complex conceptual schemas). Put another way, what cannot be imagined cannot be chosen by the individual. Communicative competence in using different language systems is essential both for conceptualization and for communicating the nature of one's choices to others. On the other hand, the range of intentional awareness, the ability to make complex interpretations, and the possibility of imagining alternative future possibilities are all restricted by limited language codes that communicate a life world of recipe knowledge. Without access to alternative interpretations of how work or technology can be organized, for example, the individual's existential choice (conscious acts of intending objects of awareness, interpreting, giving meaning, imagining) will be restricted to the givens of the existing social order, and the transcendent nature of consciousness will remain unrealized and unexpressed for lack of conceptual ability. The sense of taken-for-grantedness about how to view progress, aging, ways of knowing, the health of our bodies and spirit, the aesthetics of socially organized space is also an important influence on the individual's inclination and capacity to make existential choices. In effect the existential possibilities of the individual are profoundly influenced both by the conceptual maps codified in the symbol systems of the culture and the level of existential commitment and awareness of the significant others who play such an instrumental role in the socialization process.

NOTES

1. Jules Henry, *Culture against Man* (New York: Vintage Books, 1963), 293.
2. Hans Peter Drietzel, ed., *Recent Sociology: Patterns of Communicative Behavior* (New York: Macmillan, 1970), 53.
3. Ibid.
4. Geoffrey Esland, *Language and Social Reality* (Bletchley, England: Open University Press, 1973), 29.
5. David E. Rumelhart, *Schemata: The Building Blocks of Cognition* (La Jolla: University of California Press, 1978), 2.
6. Edward T. Hall, *Beyond Culture* (Garden City, N.Y.: Anchor Books, 1977), 44.
7. Michel Foucault, *The Order of Things* (New York: Vintage Books, 1973), *xx*.
8. Hall, *Beyond Culture*, 43.

9. Anselm Strauss, *George Herbert Mead on Social Psychology* (Chicago: University of Chicago Press, 1964), 202.
10. Peter Berger and Thomas Luckmann, *The Social Construction of Reality* (Garden City, N.Y.: Anchor Books, 1967), 37.

3

Understanding the Power
of the Teacher

The configuration of beliefs and values underlying modern culture is
fundamentally at odds with the process of socialization I have just examined. Whereas the modernizing mode of consciousness upholds the view
that the new can be understood on its own terms, the theory of socialization points to the fact that our conceptual frameworks, language, and
even personal sense of identity, in being shaped by traditional patterns
of thought, reproduces the deep conceptual patterns of the past. The
ideology of modernizing consciousness says, in effect, that we can take
control and direct our own future; what we understand about the process
of socialization tells us that we are unconscious carriers of our past. Stated
simply, even though the ideology of modernization tells us that as rational
individuals we can free ourselves from the past, the process of socialization remains a fundamentally conservative process. Even the bedrock
beliefs and values of modern consciousness reproduce the deepest
patterns of Western thought.

   A theory of education must take seriously the values and assumptions
that have produced modern consciousness, but it must also be grounded
in an understanding of how socialization both binds us to the past while
at the same time providing the basis of individual thought. This is not to
suggest that educational theory must be grounded in what appears as a
basic contradiction. The contradiction is not real, only an illusion of the
ideology that dichotomizes social reality in a way that separates the
present from the past and the individual from cultural tradition that is
sustained in the language of everyday conversation. A theory of education
that is grounded in an understanding of how our patterns of thought are
acquired will enable the teacher to understand which "moves" in the
language game of socialization are likely to bind the student to the world

of taken-for-granted belief and which "moves" enable the student to obtain conceptual distance necessary for reflective thought. When learning was based on what teachers interpreted to be the "experience" of the student, there was a general lack of understanding of the relationship between culture (as reflected in the curriculum), language (the communication processes going on in the classroom), and consciousness (the student's conceptual framework). Because the metaphor of "experience" lacked the explanatory power to illuminate the teacher's influence on the role of language in reproducing the collective culture in the consciousness of the student, there was a shift in educational thought to considering "behavior" as the primary indicator of learning. This new metaphor, which reflected the ascendency of positivistic thought, enabled educators to focus greater attention on controlling environmental factors, but it prevented them from considering the interaction of the social, linguistic, and conceptual processes that occur in the classroom. The sociology of knowledge provides, as was shown in the last chapter, the conceptual means for understanding the student's world of experience, including why the student is often unaware of many cultural messages that are being learned at a tacit level. The sociology of knowledge, with its emphasis on communication and social actors, helps to see the social environment as a source of reinforcement, which is the major concern of the behaviorists. But the sociology of knowledge provides a means of understanding the educational process in a way that does not separate behavior from the conceptual and experience from its linguistic and cultural roots. In effect, by illuminating how language reproduces the belief system of society in the consciousness of the student the sociology of knowledge provides the basic concepts necessary for a prescriptive theory of education that leads to communicative competence. Its potential thus goes beyond simply describing how schools, as distributors of culture, help maintain the class divisions of society.

Before examining the concepts that the sociology of knowledge makes available for understanding the dynamics of socialization that occur as teacher and students interact in the classroom, it would be useful to identify what distinguishes socialization in school from what occurs in the social world outside the school. The covert curriculum of school routines and behavioral norms is an important aspect of socialization, but it is the curriculum of textbooks, teacher talk, and lesson plans that deserves special attention. The unique influence of the organized school curriculum on the socialization of the student can be more clearly seen by making a distinction between the functional knowledge of the culture which the student acquires through the normal processes of interacting with others and the symbolic knowledge of culture that is acquired through the curriculum. The distinction is not meant to be an absolute one because the student's functional knowledge of how to operate in the social world obviously involves acquiring a facility in using the symbolic knowledge that underlies the different communication systems the individual uses. But the distinction serves to emphasize the degree of control the school exerts through its capacity to select, legitimatize, and reinforce the symbolic knowledge that enable students to organize conceptually the everyday world of experience.

Perhaps the distinction between functional and symbolic knowledge of culture can be seen more clearly in terms of the different kinds of learning the student undergoes. When most students go to school for the first time they already possess a functional knowledge of much of the culture that enables them to negotiate successfully a wide range of socially expected behaviors. They will have undoubtedly learned, among other things, how to compete for attention, to manage social distance and eye contact when communicating with others, to be cooperative, to regulate important biological and social functions in accordance with mechanical time, and to interact with a wide range of technological phenomena— talking on the telephone, switching on the lights, playing with toys, and so on. Socialization to the cultural codes that regulate these experiences is functional in that the child not only acquires the taken-for-granted ways of perceiving social situations (i.e., behaviors appropriate to sitting at the table, how to form up in a line, etc.) but also experience in carrying out social performances under the guidance of others. In effect, successful socialization leaves the child with the increased capacity to perform behaviorally in a manner congruent with the expectations of others. Through interaction with a wide range of significant others, the child acquires an operational or functional understanding of how to think and act in a variety of social situations. Thus the functional knowledge is learned through immediate experiences involving the guidance of others, it involves real social consequences that serve as indicators of whether one has carried out successfully the social performance as defined by others, and it can be understood as a tacit form of knowledge in that the individual's natural attitude towards the process of learning results in not being explicitly aware of much of what has been learned. It is, in essence, a form of knowledge that involves being able to carry out successful social performances that the individual may not be able to conceptualize in an explicit, rational manner. Acquiring functional knowledge is really a case of learning more than we can articulate and in many cases, even acknowledge. It can also be understood as the primary form of socialization that will be continued in the adult world.

Much of the socialization carried on in schools involves acquiring a functional knowledge of the cultural norms appropriate to life in the classroom. Behaviors appropriate for asking questions, establishing one's identity through competitive performance, relating to the schedules of the school, moving through both social and physical spaces, interacting with the opposite sex, all serve as familiar examples of this form of socialization, which will be later replicated countless times as the student enters the world of adults. It represents the covert curriculum that has attracted considerable interest in recent years.

But this is not the primary function of schools, nor does it represent the unique form of socialization that separates schools from the rest of social life. What is unique about the form of socialization the school has been assigned to carry on relates to its role as a transmitter of symbolic knowledge. Through contact with the received curriculum students acquire the institutionally sanctioned words, concepts, and theoretical frameworks that will enable them to conceptualize many of the experiences that have been the source of their tacit, functional knowledge. For example, while students have already learned to function in different work settings around the home they will acquire through the curriculum the vocabulary and concepts for thinking about the organization and value orientation of the work process. This is achieved by learning the socially shared typifications which often represent an ideal or, at least, simplified image. A similar example is the student who has already learned, at the functional level, how to operate within the complex set of social relationships of the family; the school will provide discussions and readings that enable the student to think and communicate about the family in a way that is socially congruent. While the student will generally have acquired some facility in the use of language as part of functional learning, the school curriculum will help to stabilize the typical interpretation of social reality embedded in the language. Thus, the student encounters a typification of a good family and by comparison, a bad family. The student will also encounter the typified way of thinking about other aspects of the culture: What time is and how it is to be used; what competition is, and how it is to be perceived as different from cooperation; what constitutes legitimate forms of knowledge; how to think about progress; what technology means, and so forth. As these typifications are internalized as part of the students' conceptual map they serve as reference points for giving meaning and making interpretations of everyday life.

The school's power to control and legitimatize the students' symbolic knowledge of culture is related to the simple fact that the primary means of representing much of the culture to the student is not through direct experience of the culture, but rather through words and visual images. Students encounter outside the classroom a depth of experience that is often not made explicit in the language that accompanies social interaction. Alfred Korzybski's observation that the "map is not the territory"[1] suggests a similar relationship between language and experience: language provides a means of mapping experience but is not the same as the experience. Through the curriculum of the school, however, students will encounter verbal descriptions of cultural experiences, and will also be conditioned to believe in many instances that the concepts reproduced in language are more accurate indicators of social reality than direct experience. Socialization in the schools emphasizes understanding culture at the symbolic level where social reality is mediated through words, concepts, and conceptual maps that provide the logic for relating one thought to another. Thus, students read about life in cities, unemployment, automation, progress, people of other cultures, and so forth. While there may be attempts to involve students in simulation, role playing, and direct observation of social life, the primary emphasis is on the acquisition of symbolic knowledge that is essential to thinking and talking (at an abstract level) about the everyday life. Vocabulary building is not an activity that is systematically promoted by any other institution except the public school; its importance to the school reflects the dominant orientation of representing the culture through words. To put it another way, the most important and pervasive activities in school are talking, listening, and reading about different aspects of the culture. Students who cannot relate to the culture at this abstract, symbolic level are not likely to succeed.

The emphasis on symbolic knowledge gives the school tremendous power to influence not only what the student will think about, but also the conceptual framework the student will use later in life. At some point in the public school curriculum nearly every aspect of the culture will be talked about; even areas of social experience that cause embarrassment and collective silence will be typified in a manner that is intended to foster (though not always successfully) a similar attitude in the student. The range of coverage makes the legitimation function of the school all the more important. The curriculum contains controlled vocabularies (reflecting both legitimate pedagogic and more questionable political concerns) that typify and thus legitimatize how the student is supposed to think. For example, students are given the explanation that *"economics* is the study of how people make and exchange things they need and want."* Automation is explained as "a new way of using machines—it is using machines to run machines."[2] As these examples demonstrate, the symbolic knowledge acquired by the student—the vocabulary that typifies how to think about social reality, the theoretical framework that serves as a conceptual map for organizing experience into meaningful patterns— often simplify, and, on occasion, even distort the complexity of the culture people live. The complex and more problematic aspects of the experience not represented in the vocabulary or explanation given to students becomes an area of "audible silence," and the public school curricula contains many such areas.

If we take seriously the connection between language and thought, which includes the influence of language on how we organize our ideas as well as what we are able to communicate to others, we can see the potential of the school to influence the thought of students. The two extremes are represented in the power of the school to socialize students to the vocabulary and conceptual framework that simply reinforces the students' stock of taken-for-granted beliefs acquired through interaction with others (including the media) and its potential for providing students with the vocabulary and conceptual frameworks that will enable the student to recognize continuities in experience and to re-conceptualize those aspects of taken-for-granted belief that can no longer be justified. Although the dependency of the student on the school is not absolute (experience leads people to continually add to their conceptual maps as well as rethink important elements) it is, nevertheless, very real. When the school provides the vocabulary and conceptual framework that further reinforces taken-for-granted beliefs, or avoids making available the language that will enable the student to name and conceptualize areas of experience that are characterized by a collective silence (including a knowledge of the past), the socialization process becomes an impediment to the development of communicative competence. In a culture that places a premium on investing explicit language codes with the power to represent reality, socialization that limits language facility (as well as a knowledge of assumptions that underlies the conceptual maps that are reproduced through language) limits the individual's power in both the existential and political sense. Knowledge and facility in using the language systems that make up the culture are, on the other hand, a source of power. The connection between language and power can be seen, historically, in the special power exercised by the priesthood, in contemporary times by ideologues and those who know the new language of the computer. The poet who wrote, "I have forgotten the word I intended to say, and my thought, embodied, returns to the realm of shadow,"[3] touches on the primacy of language in making choice a possibility for the individual. That we think in the language of others makes the question of power doubly problematic.

In addition to socializing students on how to think about their culture as opposed to learning from direct experience, the school performs another function that adds to the uniqueness of its form of socialization. Sociological studies of the relationship between language and social stratification, particularly the work done by Basil Bernstein and Pierre Bourdieu,[4] point to the crucial gatekeeper role that has been assigned to schools. What these studies have shown is that there is a direct connection between language and social class, and that the schools use language facility as the basis of deciding which students will be given access to the credentials necessary for higher status jobs. Schools do not provide equality of opportunity because students possess, at the time of entry, unequal facility with the medium used by teachers to determine the student's success. Neo-Marxist educators have further developed the analysis to show that economics, specifically the capitalistic form of economics, underlies the class divisions that are maintained through the school curriculum and assessment practices.

While their analyses of the school's role in maintaining the hegemonic culture is particularly powerful, the neo-Marxists have been unable to develop a theory of education that addresses the broader educational goals (i.e., whether a liberal education has a place in the world they envisage) or the specifics of what teachers should do in the classroom. The inability to find within Marxism a clear sense of direction for the reform of educational practice can be seen in the varied and often contradictory reform proposals that individual Marxists have supported. Some neo-Marxist educational theorists have argued for a radical deschooling of society, others have outlined proposals that are sympathetic to progressive and even neoromantic educational practices, while others have come full circle by supporting the view that capitalist society can only be overturned if students receive access to the traditional forms of liberal education associated with bourgeois culture.[5]

Since Marxist theory does not lead to a specific educational practice I will have to return to the Schutz, Berger, and Luckmann stream of the sociology of knowledge in order to find the theoretical basis for articulating a theory of education that prepares students to live in an increasingly politicized world. Another reason for returning to the theoretical framework of Schutz, Berger, and Luckmann is that their view of socialization avoids the romantic view of the non-repressive life that people are supposed to live after the revolution. Primary socialization does not fit the vision of a society free of domination and inequality, as the process of socialization itself involves a fundamental form of domination as the significant other gives the person undergoing socialization the language (and conceptual map) for naming and thinking about the social world.

Although the teacher's influence on student attitudes, self-concept, and academic achievement is now generally understood, there has been less attention given to the teacher's control over whether socialization transmits the belief system at the level of taken-for-granted beliefs or enables the student to obtain the conceptual distance (including historical perspective) essential for critical reflection. The failure in recent years to consider whether the teacher's style of pedagogy liberates the mind is in part a result of the general eclipse of the idea of a liberalizing education by the technocratic orientation that emphasizes a highly systematized approach to teaching basic skills. The neoromantic and neo-Marxists have been obsessed with eliminating both the authoritarian role of the teacher and the influence of tradition on the curriculum, but for different reasons. Their efforts, however, have led to the same results, namely, a general sense of indifference, if not hostility, toward taking seriously the liberalizing influence that the teacher has on the process of learning.

Aside from the silence created by these different streams of educational thought that are in conflict with each other on surface issues, but share in common the deeper level categories and assumptions that are the bedrock of modern consciousness, there is a more fundamental reason why so little attention has been given to the power of the teacher to influence how the student learns the culture transmitted through the curriculum. In order to talk about whether education is liberating or not, it is necessary to talk about human consciousness. Until fairly recently we have lacked a knowledge of the theoretical frameworks that would enable us to do this. With the rise of interest in the work of Piaget, the growing interest in the European tradition of phenomenology, and the parallel body of work being done by cognitive psychologists and sociologists that focuses on how cognition is influenced by social interaction, we now have conceptual tools for talking about the relationship between the culture transmitted by curriculum, the language environment within the classroom, and the influence of social processes on human consciousness. These tools of analysis enable us to break with the positivistic world of an atomistic individual and objective knowledge, which led so easily to talking about objective knowledge, education inputs, and learning as a product. These new conceptual tools also enable us to take seriously the influence of the teacher on the consciousness of the student. In effect, the work in the area of what Hugh Mehan called "social constructionism,"[6] which includes the sociology of knowledge of Schutz, Berger, and Luckmann, provides words for naming and thus thinking about aspects of experience that have been forced into the shadows by theorists who have insisted on dealing only with what can be observed. Now that the structure and processes of human consciousness is being rescued from the academic Gulag, it is also possible to take seriously again the problem of a liberalizing pedagogy.

If we keep in mind that what goes on in the language environment of the classroom is too complex to be reduced to a categorical judgment, we can nevertheless ask whether the dynamics of cultural transmission carried on by the teacher contributes to the student's ability to think and communicate more effectively or binds the student to a world of taken-for-granted belief where behavior and thought are culturally dictated. To put the question more simply: What should the teacher understand about the relationship between culture, language, and human consciousness? Without an understanding of this relationship, the teacher will be unable to adjust the style of pedagogy in a manner that would give control over whether the culture is being communicated to students at an explicit or an implicit level. Both levels of communication have their appropriate moments, but in terms of whether the teacher is knowledgeable about the effects of different styles of pedagogy, and the political consequences faced later by the student who cannot escape the hold of taken-for-granted beliefs, it is imperative that the teacher possess the means of understanding the dynamics of the socialization process in which they are involving the student.

If we return to the primary level of socialization where students are encountering for the first time a new element in their social world—how to ask a question, how to think about the organization of work, how to define a researchable problem, and so on—we find that students are in a dependent relationship with the significant other (teacher) who is a carrier of the social knowledge that is the basis of the socialization process. A brief review of the dynamics of the relationship between the student and teacher will help bring into focus the typical "moves" in the language game of socialization and will suggest alternative "moves." By keeping in mind that the pedagogical relationship is simply another way of describing the socialization of students we can see the options that are available to the teacher. An awareness of the following questions lead to recognizing that the teacher can change the process, and thus the outcome, of socialization

Does the Content of the Curriculum Reflect What the Student Already Experiences as Taken for Granted?

As stated earlier, much of the curriculum, as well as the teaching process itself reflects the transmission of "unconscious culture." In the language of the sociology of knowledge, this "unconscious culture" represents the taken-for-granted beliefs that guide the conduct of everyday life. The feelings of naturalness and inevitability that accompanies taken-for-granted attitudes insures that much of what gets communicated in social settings, including classrooms, will serve as the social recipes that give continuity and predictability to social life. This sense of the social world as nonproblematic leads to a non-questioning attitude toward the deeper cultural codes which underlie the organization of the social-cognitive world of the individual. As so much of the culture is transmitted and stabilized in consciousness at this tacit level of awareness, it is inevitable that much of the content of the curriculum will reflect the taken-for-granted beliefs of textbook writers, selection committees, teachers, and local school boards. Although not all taken-for-granted beliefs are undesirable, the pedagogical problem arises because some of the definitions, beliefs, and assumptions that make up the world view teachers share with students no longer make sense in terms of what we now understand about social and ecological problems. The unique challenge for the teacher and curriculum developer is to determine which taken-for-granted beliefs need to be made explicit and examined, and this is difficult because they must first be problematized before their merit can be judged. The difficulty in being aware of what needs to be problematized can be seen in the sexist and racist stereotypes naively communicated until recently in textbooks at the level of taken-for-granted belief. The problematic nature of these taken-for-granted beliefs was not discovered by educators until after sexism and racism had been debated and generally condemned by the larger society. The problem of making explicit what we tend to take for granted makes it all the more imperative that the teacher be sensitive to this aspect of the socialization process.

For students, encountering significant areas of culture under the guidance of teachers and curriculum developers who are unable to pose significant questions or point to important relationships because the sense of taken-for-grantedness closes off other conceptual possibilities, can shape significantly the direction of their lives. The process will leave the middle-class student, whose recipe knowledge has been further buttressed by institutional legitimation, without the conceptual tools necessary for reconstituting those aspects of the recipe knowledge that are likely to be frayed and challenged by social events that the recipe knowledge was not designed to explain. The underlying assumptions of the culture now being problematized by the ecological crisis—assumptions that shape our thinking in a manner that anthropomorthizes the world, and causes us to view science and technology as talismen that will cause problems to disappear—points to the need for the middle class, including its youth, to acquire the symbolic tools necessary for making explicit and reformulating those aspects of the dominant belief system that are contributing to the problems we face. For youth who possess a different cultural background, the encounter with the taken-for-granted beliefs of the dominant society is both a confusing and demeaning experience that may leave them with a diminished competence to communicate about either their own cultural experience or the dominant one that is presented as a powerful and mystifying referent for judging who they are. For both groups of students, learning the taken-for-granted beliefs leaves them with a diminished competence to communicate about either their own cultural experience or the dominant one that is presented as a powerful and mystifying referent for judging who they are. For both groups of students, learning the taken-for-granted beliefs leaves them with restricted vocabularies and limited capacity for negotiating new definitions and understandings. To use Paulo Freire's phrase, they are being socialized to a "culture of silence" where existence will be defined by external sources they will not understand or be able to challenge.

How social reality is actually represented in the curriculum needs to be analyzed more carefully, and to do this it will be necessary to map the areas of belief that are presented as taken-for-granted reality. As educators become aware of what is being represented as taken for granted they will be able to see more clearly those areas of consensus belief, grounded in the habituated thinking of the past, that must be problematized. The core beliefs and assumptions of the culture—our way of thinking about work, technology, efficiency, ways of knowing, authority, progress, space, and time—are particularly important as they shape our institutions, patterns of daily life, and self-identity. They also represent the part of the Western epistemology most related to the development of our technocratic-commodity culture whose future is now so much in doubt. By problematizing relevant areas of consensus belief by making them explicit and subjecting them to analysis, the educator will be helping students acquire the more complex language codes necessary for acting as a conscious agent in a process where change must take account of cultural continuities that deserve to be maintained. In considering the significance of making explicit taken-for-granted beliefs, it is important to recall the previous discussion of how limited language codes constrain thought and imagination and serve politically to reinforce the definitions of reality that fit other people's taken-for-granted beliefs. It should also be recalled how concerned people were when they suddenly discovered that sexist and racist attitudes were being communicated in classrooms as the taken-for-granted reality on which everyday life was based. Hopefully, this sense of concern can be extended to other areas of the collective belief system that are shaped by the school's power to control and legitimatize the symbolic codes that serve as the conceptual patterns for guiding experience.

Mapping areas of taken-for-granted belief should enable us to see where, in terms of age level, important concepts, definitions and assumptions are introduced and to assess more clearly if they are dealt with later in the student's career at a more sophisticated and explicit level. For example, some of the most basic assumptions and definitions are introduced in the elementary grades (e.g., the nature of time, modernity, technology, work, ways of knowing, etc). An important question relates to whether the taken-for-granted ways of perceiving these aspects of the culture are ever dealt with directly at a later stage in the educational process, or if they are ignored because they represent such a basic core of taken-for-granted beliefs that nobody bothers to consider them as important. It would also be useful to explore the articulation (or lack of it) between what prospective teachers learn about the deep epistemic codes underlying their culture and the concepts they are expected to teach at each grade level. A cursory examination of the elementary curriculum reveals that students learn how to think about time, work, technology, modernity, poverty, to list a few of the curriculum units. If prospective teachers do not study these important areas of their culture in any systematic manner, either in their professional or liberal arts courses, then we have to ask where they get the knowledge necessary for teaching about such important areas of the collective belief system. As elementary teachers they are not likely to deal with the deep structure of these beliefs and assumptions in most college courses designated as part of the teacher training program, consequently they must either rely upon information supplied in the teacher's manual or simply fall back on their own taken-for-granted understanding of work, technology, or whatever else is being discussed in the classroom. In either case, the student is likely to encounter simplistic interpretations, a limited vocabulary that contains typifications that deproblematizes the part of the culture being studied, and reinforcement from the teacher for internalizing into his or her explanatory framework the teacher's recipe knowledge. Unfortunately the teacher's influence on the student's symbolic knowledge of culture is not a primary concern of teacher-training institutions. If it were, more attention would be given to the question of whether prospective teachers, particularly in the elementary grades, have an adequate understanding of the culture they will otherwise naively communicate to students.

Is the Content of the Curriculum Represented as Reified Reality?

The process of ideas and values taking on the quality of objective reality has been a traditional concern within the sociology of knowledge. As Peter Berger and Stanley Pullberg have observed,[7] it is anthropologically necessary for people to communicate their ideas to others in a manner that creates the shared world we know as culture. This process of externalization transforms what was a subjective reality into an objectified, socially shared reality. As a human product, it often takes on a sense of "thingness" and evolves its own social history. Ideas like Darwin's theory of natural selection, Rousseau's romantic notions about human nature, and the Enlightenment ideas of reason and equality are good examples. An example closer to each of us would be the utterance we casually make that takes on a life of its own that are interpreted by others and perhaps even recorded in some form of public record. Even though we may later disown it, it often survives as something objectively real. Berger and Pullberg, as well as others in the sociology of knowledge field, have identified alienation with the process of forgetting that the products of man (ideas, rules, institutions, values, interpretations, etc.) have a human authorship. The moment of forgetting or losing sight of the human authorship they call reification. What is experienced as reified takes on the character of thinghood and appears as objectively real. The concept of reification is perhaps one of the most useful analytical tools available for understanding the socialization process that goes on in the classroom. It is important because it provides a means for examining the significance of presenting students with explanations, ideas, beliefs, and values that appear to be ontologically indepedent of human authorship. The concept also helps to understand how reifications are sustained through the reality constituting process of communication, as well as how they undermine the individual's power to negotiate new definitions of reality.

Analyzing the curriculum for the purpose of identifying the presence of reifications may at first be difficult because the very nature of a reification makes it difficult to see. Often the reification is embedded in the language that both shapes our thought and serves as the medium for communicating with others. For example, the categories that lead us to organize our thoughts into the patterns of "either-or," "cause-effect," "right-wrong" are reifications. A reified belief is coercive in that it directs thought in a particular way; at the same time it is experienced as both inevitable and a natural part of reality. A way of helping to make reifications stand out more clearly is to keep in mind that social reality, ideas, values, norms, rules, institutions (all that makes up culture), is a human construction; social reality is reified when it does not appear to have human authorship. The following observations by Peter Berger and Thomas Luckmann may serve as useful guides.

> Reification implies that man is capable of forgetting his own authorship of the human world. . . . The reified world is, by definition, a de-humanized world. . . . The objectivity of the social world means that it confronts man as something outside of himself. The decisive question is whether he still retains the awareness that, however objectified, the social world was made by men—and, therefore, can be remade by them. . . . typically, the real relationship between man and his world is reversed in consciousness. . . . That is, man is capable paridoxically of producing a reality that denies him.[8]

Berger and Luckmann's description of reification applies to the world of public education. Test scores, as well as the need to use specific forms of testing, stand out as important examples of reifications. Rules, schedules, and degree requirements tend to take on the quality of "thingness," with the consequence that people lose sight of the fact that they have the power to change them when they cease to serve a useful purpose. The reified world of education can also include theories of learning like behaviorism, the roles of teachers and administrators, and individual identities that include both teachers and students. How the reifications in the educational process affect the psychological development of individuals and influence learning have only recently been studied. Our purpose here, however, is to focus briefly on the reified content of the curriculum in order to examine its influence on the socialization of students.

As much of the reality sharing process of the curriculum is dependent on written language there is a greater tendency for reification than if socialization were dependent entirely on interpersonal communication. This does not mean that interpersonal communication is free of reifications; what is being stressed here is that the nature of our language contributes to the transformation within the communication process of subjective intentions and interpretations into statements that often appear to denote an objective reality. Our subject-predicate form of speech creates, according to Clyde Kluckhohn, the appearance of a changeless world of fixed relations between "substances" and their "qualities."[9] The appearance of facticity—that things are as they are named—is achieved by the inadequacy of our language to communicate context, intentionality, and subjective meaning. Statements about social reality tend to take on the quality of objective reporting and as they are communicated to others or put in print their human authorship is generally obscured. As the conventions of our language objectify what is being communicated reification becomes inevitable.

Every subject area of the curriculum has its reification, generally embedded in the "reporting" style characteristic of the manner in which most textbooks and curriculum materials are written. An examination of science curricula will reveal the reification of the mode of knowing that separates the knowner from the object of perception. In addition to sustaining the reifications of positivism, students also encounter reifications that fuse scientific inquiry with truth and progress. Many of the categories for organizing knowledge, as well as the laws that were first advanced as working hypotheses, are communicated to students in reified form. In the area of physical education, the body has been reified, as well as the ideas of competition and winning. Art education has its own set of reifications, including the ideas of individual creativity and art as a product. The areas of language arts and literature transmit the reifications that have served to govern style, format and content of written expansion, as well as the interpretations of literary efforts that have themselves become reified and constraining.

The reifications in social science curricula tend to be more obvious than in other areas of the school curricula, perhaps because our general awareness of the complexity of the social world provides a reference point that enables us to see the reifications transmitted in the classroom. The way of typifying efficiency, poverty, and progress, which was cited earlier, serve as typical examples. What the student reads in the textbook about the division of labor serves as an example of the pervasiveness of the reified beliefs communicated as the taken-for-granted way of perceiving reality: "The way these workers do their job is called *division of labor. Division* is a word that means 'act of splitting something into parts.' *Labor* means the unit it takes to get a job done. So *division of labor* means 'each worker does a part of the job.'"[10] The reification of the division of labor cuts the student off from seeing the necessity of understanding the history of how craftsmanship evolved under the influence of purposive rationality and the profit motive into the segmented activity we now call labor. This example also shows how the reification of part of our belief system tends to de-problematize what has been reified by keeping it isolated from existential experience. As a reification it obfuscates its historical roots while at the same time claiming its independence from the need to be validated in personal experience. Like in the textbook statement "Healthy cities are like boys and girls. They grow bigger and bigger," reifications of the social world become, for many students, the conceptual building blocks for orientating themselves in an otherwise indeterminate world. Experience thus becomes symbolized in a manner that reverses the relationship between experience and abstract thought, with the consequence that abstract thought becomes the reality and actual experience becomes only an epiphenomenon.

In suggesting that educators should become more aware of reifications in the curriculum, it is necessary to keep in mind both their pervasiveness and the difficulty in detecting them. There is also a judgment that must be made about which reifications are more important in terms of influencing the quality of individual and social life. The educator cannot detect and problematize all reifications in the curriculum; therefore, the educator needs to have an understanding of the more significant social developments in order to make a judgment about which aspect of the collective reified consciousness are most in need of problematizing. The process of socializing students to the reified beliefs held by others is directly related to the question of whether education will lead to greater communicative competence or to a form of mystification that undermines the student's power to reconceptualize important areas of social reality. The idea of communicative competence involves the ability to problematize taken-for-granted experience as a necessary step in becoming culturally literate. Cultural literacy, in turn, leads to the level of understanding that enables one to call into question the underlying assumption that gives social experience its particular characteristics. This process, which is essential to the cultural changes we have witnessed recently in the feminist movement, enables the individual to actively participate in the reconstruction of social reality. The nature of reified beliefs, on the other hand, has the opposite effect of causing the individual to feel powerless both existentially and conceptually to challenge the reality that appears independent of human authorship.

As I will discuss later, the process of de-reification should not involve pre-figured positions where the teacher substitutes a new reification for the outmoded one. If a belief or value exists as a reification, it will first have to be brought to the level of explicit awareness and examined before judgments can be made about social worth. This process will enable both the student and teacher to see new relationships between the reified belief, its historical origins, and its relation to current social problems; and the process will lead to a more complex language code for conceptualizing and communicating about that area of social experience. If teachers short circuit this process by substituting the reifications of their own ideology the student will be left without the conceptual tools necessary for genuine understanding.

What Are the Areas of Audible Silence in the Curriculum?

An analysis of the curriculum should be sensitive to those areas of social and individual experience that are not presented in the curriculum—areas of human experience about which there is a collective silence in the larger society due either to a lack of communicative competence in focusing and articulating the issues or to the fear that often arises when it is no longer possible to escape existential choices forced on us by critical awareness. Alvin Gouldner has referred to this phenomenon in terms of "audible silence." This phrase is important because it suggests an existential awareness that is not communicated because society is unprepared to deal with it. It is not like the silence associated with taken-for-granted beliefs; this form of silence does not involve suppressed awareness or a tension between experience and a belief system. When experience is taken for granted, there is no awareness of alternative definitions or values. The experience is simply part of the natural order of things (e.g., ideas may be experienced as privately owned, women seen as less capable than men, technological inventiveness as a sign of progress, etc.). *Audible silence*, on the other hand, refers to those areas of experience where there is an awareness that is not, for one reason or another, communicated.

In terms of the socialization of students, the educator has an obligation to insure that the curriculum does not confront the student with the audible silence experienced in the larger society. This obligation cannot, of course, involve teachers in a Promethian role of bringing insights and truth to students which exceed their own level of awareness. What it does involve is an awareness that the school is one institution where students *might* have the opportunity to put into a broader historical and social perspective those aspects of existential experience that are not explained adequately by the dominant belief system. It also involves an awareness that in order to think about experience, whether it relates to work, ways of knowing, competitions, authority, or the like, the student will need a language code that does more than transmit the society's taken-for-granted assumptions.

A cursory examination of classroom curriculum materials reveals examples of audible silence that should not escape the notice of people responsible for curriculum decisions. Curriculum materials dealing with career education serve as an example. The vocabulary to be learned by students in a seventh grade classroom is designed to describe a world of work that is free of stress, alientation, exploitation, or any kind of complexity. Students learn about being "thorough," "tactful," or "punctual," but there is no vocabulary for thinking about the discontents associated with the different kinds of work available in our society. Nor are concepts made available that might enable students to think of alternate ways of organizing work. Like the workers Richard Sennett and Jonathan Cobb interviewed in *The Hidden Injuries of Class*, the students who encounter the work ideology presented in most curricula dealing with career education will be unable to articulate why some forms of work will cause them to view themselves as inferior, powerless individuals. The discontents and complexities of work (e.g., the feeling of being powerless to control one's work while at the same time needing self-respect; the tension between the need for fraternity and the job-related imperative for judging the competency of a fellow worker) represent areas of audible silence in the curriculum. Teaching students to think of technology as the wellspring that gives us the commodity culture we have learned to associate with progress and the good life, without also teaching them how technology has influenced our most basic ways of thinking, is another example. Thinking about machines has, over the past two centuries, resulted in thinking in metaphors derived from the world of machines, which is reflected in a vocabulary that uses word such as components, interface, input, output, reproducibility, systems, or feedback. In being socialized to the cognitive style of technocratic consciousness, students will be faced with situations in which they may sense but not be able to articulate why their mode of thought is inappropriate for responding to certain human problems. The student who has not been encouraged to explore the tension between creativity and technique may later experience the audible silence of the art education curriculum in a manner similar to the student who has not been given the concepts, vocabulary, and alternative perspectives necessary for thinking about the aesthetics of social spaces. They will move through social space without understanding the underlying language systems that make some experiences pleasing and restful, and others discomforting. Nor are they likely to understand the tension between routinization and self-expression.

In recent years, progress has been made in helping students examine areas of social experience that previously were not discussed openly in public. Sex education, sexism, racism, and attitudes toward aging and death are among the more important examples. But much of our cultural experience is still not being talked about directly, either in the home or in scholastic institutions, even though these topics affects in the most profound way the quality of daily life. The social and existential consequences of competition, the positivistic mode of thinking, the effects of a dominating concern with profit, the utilization of nonrenewable resources in the name of progress, the qualitative distinction between a collective and a community, the tension between the need for sanctity and feeling of power associated with an anthropocentric view of the world, are among the issues that should be discussed in a setting free of slogans and predetermined answers. The selection of topics will vary depending on the imagination and background of the teacher and what seems most relevant to the existential needs of the students. But the selection should be guided by an awareness that what is not talked about becomes a powerful determinant in shaping thought. For without the tools of language that make reflexive thought possible, socialization can channel and limit thought particularly in those areas of experience where explanatory systems are not held existentially and politically accountable by being tested against actual experience.

Is the Curriculum Characterized by a Limited or Complex Language Code?

The use of a sociology of knowledge theory as a basis for analyzing school curricula as a reality constituting process helps to clarify the fundamental importance in the socialization process and the unique control the school exercises over language acquisition. Since I have already discussed both the reality constituting and sustaining characteristics of language and the school's control of symbolic knowledge, I will focus briefly on the importance of teachers and curriculum developers being aware of whether the content of the curriculum is communicated in a limited or a complex language code. An analysis of the curriculum's language code may be one of the most effective means of identifying statements that are reified or represented as taken-for-granted reality. If students are presented a limited vocabulary and set of concepts for thinking about an area of cultural experience, the teacher should understand immediately the likely effects this will have on their ability to re-think the recipe formulations they have been given. Essentially, the teacher should ask two questions about the language in a curriculum unit: (1) Is the vocabulary and conceptual schema sufficiently complex to communicate to students, at a level they can understand, the actual complexity of what is being studied? (2) Does the language reveal either the human authorship or the social perspective of the person who wrote the materials being used in the curriculum material? Sensitivity to the importance of asking these two questions should help teachers exercise more thoughtful control over important aspects of the socialization process and hopefully contribute to the student's power to understand.

Does Socialization Involve Using the Legitimation Process to Make Students Feel Powerless?

The process of primary socialization carried on through classroom conversation may possess another characteristic that contributes to socialization becoming a matter of reproducing in the mind of students the conceptual maps of the teacher. Just as many of the "moves" in the language game of socialization are carried out unconsciously by the teacher, there is the possibility that the teacher will outmaneuver the student who questions by escalating the level of legitimating authority. The teacher's need to define what authority is may be rooted in a world view that has become an integral part of the teacher's self-concept. Student questioning of what is being explained by the teacher may thus not only be disturbing to the teacher because it challenges taken-for-granted beliefs, but may also threaten to challenge the authority of the conceptual maps on which the teacher's self-concept has been built. The need to outmaneuver the student in a language game that could easily move into liminal space where new definitions for "what is" could be established may also result from the teacher's feelings of what Nietzsche called ressentiment. Simply stated, ressentiment involves the inability to openly recognize the limitation of one's own position when challenged by a superior source of authority. The ressentient teacher can use the different levels of legitimation as a way of protecting a personally held position without facing a direct encounter with the source of the threat. In most instances, however, it is likely that the teacher uses the different levels of legitimation to insure that their explanations prevail because that was how they were socialized. In these instances, the use of the higher levels of legitimation reflect the ideological orientation that characterizes how authority is established in the university environment where teachers receive their training.

The invoking of authority to justify the explanations that are part of introducing students to new cultural territory involves a process of escalation from folk knowledge through the level of theory which reaches the highest level in the overarching cosmological explanation.[11] The first level of legitimation is expressed in the process of giving the student the vocabulary for naming "what is" (e.g., how to think about time, competition, causality, and so forth). The teacher's natural attitude toward the content of the primary socialization process is communicated as a model for how the student should relate to what is being defined as real; this is also part of the first stage of legitimation. When students, because of different perspective, conceptual maps, or questioning attitude, challenge the teacher's explanation of "what is," it is possible to move the level of legitimation to folk tradition. At this level, the authority of folk knowledge and practices can be used as a source of consensus that can overwhelm the independent position the student may be attempting to establish. If the student persists by rejecting the legitimating authority of folk traditions, the teacher can move to the level of theory. At this level of legitimation, authority is established through a rational process where success becomes largely a function of who possesses the more complex language code and thus can move from one theoretical framework to another, establish the connections between the world of theory and experience, and marshall evidence and data to buttress analysis. If the student is undergoing primary socialization, which means encountering an area of the social world for the first time, it is unlikely that the student would possess the language code necessary for participating on equal terms with the teacher whose vocation is spent transmitting the culture to students at the level of talk, theory, and world view.

Should the student continue to question the theoretical foundations of authority, the teacher can move to the highest level of legitimation involving either religious or secular based mythologies. At this level resistance to the teacher's explanations of "what is" becomes an act of heresy that few students are capable of committing or defending. For example, when "progress" or "rationalism" are invoked to justify thinking in a certain way, few students will possess sufficient knowledge or the language competency to challenge the teacher on either intellectual or moral grounds.

The irony is that these series of "moves" in the language game undermine the development of communicative competence that the educational process is supposed to foster. The students' ability to establish their own intellectual position in the face of the teacher's power to escalate the levels of legitimation requires the communicative competence that is being undermined through the misuse of power. The fact that the student is often unable to participate in the language game of socialization points to the essential political nature of socialization and to the role of language in this process. What is named often becomes what is "real," and the person who names "reality" becomes the source of control.

Students are not always dependent upon the primary socialization that teachers have planned. They often have a different set of "significant others," and in many instances their conceptual maps lead them to interpret what the teacher communicates in ways that are quite unanticipated. Even when the student undergoes primary socialization, that is, accepts the significant other's explanations of "what is," future experiences and conflicting explanations will lead to re-thinking of acquired conceptual frameworks. While socialization is not deterministic, it can nevertheless exert a powerful hold over thought and social action. Students who were socialized to sex-specific behaviors and attitudes tended to reproduce in their adult lives the conceptual schemas acquired as part of their primary socialization. Many of us still think of change as progress, organize the social structure of work in a hierarchial pattern, think of cause and effect as a linear relationship, and view thought as an individual matter. The point is that primary socialization provides the first vocabulary and conceptual schema for organizing both thought and action. Since much of the learning and teaching is tacit, the student is not always aware of the relationship between power and knowledge. To be able to express a thought appears as an expression of individual agency; that thought may be a predictable expression of the acquired conceptual schema is not likely to be recognized in an ideological environment that celebrates "self-expression," and freedom.

Does the Curriculum Contribute to Social Stratification and Inequalities of Opportunity?

Reification and the sense of taken-for-grantedness often hide one of the more important questions relating to the content of the curriculum. Reification creates the illusion of an objective, independent reality, and taken-for-granted beliefs dull the capacity for critical judgment. The questions often obscured by both reification and recipe knowledge relates to the issue of whose knowledge is transmitted through the curriculum. This is the fundamentally important question that Michael Young focused on with such precision. One of the insights of the sociology of knowledge is that social reality is a human construct; consequently all knowledge is seen as having human authorship. The loss of historical memory that characterizes conventional belief and the objectifying function of language help to obscure this fact. The recognition of the human authorship of knowledge leads to other questions relating to the social origin of knowledge and the social interests that it serves. As both Young and Apple have noted, knowledge is not neutral. It serves social purposes and special interests. Unfortunately, most teachers today, trained to think of themselves as neutral public servants seeking the best technological solution rather than as educators concerned with the truth claims of what they are asked to teach, lack the conceptual tools for demystifying the dominant view that maintains that knowledge is socially neutral. In order to see through this popular myth, the teacher would also have to challenge the positivist view of knowledge which is legitimated by the technocratic mode of consciousness that now prevails at all levels of the public bureaucracy, including the university. This is particularly important because positivism lends its own form of legitimation to the idea that knowledge is socially neutral. Challenging positivism, particularly within the university setting, is a lonely and formidable challenge indeed.

But responsible teachers and curriculum developers can begin to challenge this part of the public and professional myopia by examining how curriculum knowledge is stratified and investigating which social groups are given access to what Michael Young has called prestige knowledge.[12] Becoming sensitive to the social and cultural factors that influence decisions about which social groups of students have access to which curricula areas is important to understanding the school's role in equipping students with the symbolic codes relevant to the different social strata in society. This adds an important dimension to understanding the reality constructing process of schooling.

Concern with the question of the relation between the organization and legitimation of knowledge in the curriculum and the patterns of social stratification poses an additional problem that confronts teachers and educational policymakers today. A curriculum organized in a manner that provides equal education for all (i.e., socialization to a common set of beliefs and assumptions about reality) may within the North American context of relative cultural pluralism deny groups that represent a definite subculture freedom of choice in maintaining their own cultural traditions. The existence of cultural pluralism, in effect, makes it difficult to reconcile equality (equal in the sense of exposure to the same curricula) with the freedom of choice that is associated with democracy. But this dilemma does not eliminate the importance of Michael Young's concern with the social stratifying effects of exposing students to different symbolic codes. The moral issues surrounding stratification within a particular cultural group still remain a major concern.

What Is the Influence of the Purposive-Rational System of Thought on the Liberalizing Potential of School Knowledge?

A fundamental question posed by the sociology of knowledge relates to the influence of ideology, particularly the technocratic ideology discussed earlier, on the organization of knowledge and the educational experience of the student. For those who experience the technological mode of thought as the taken-for-granted reality, the question will seem either unimaginable as a serious question or as subversive to what they see as progress, modernization, and truth. Educators who have sufficiently kept in touch with their existential selves to realize the limitations of technological consciousness should find the question of paramount importance to understanding what is happening in the classroom.

The influence of the technological mode of thought on the organization of curriculum can be seen in the use of competency-based teaching, the commercially produced learning packages, and the systems approach to curriculum development that involve the rational pre-figuring of the relationship between content, thought processes, and behavioral outcomes. It is expressed in a concern with efficiency, predictability, and control; its basic mode of manifestation is in organizing learning packages through which the student will be processed. Curriculum materials, organized in accordance with this mind set, are thus conceptualized in terms of components that must be rationally organized as subsystems articulated to other subsystems that together make up the curriculum unit. Dividing both a field of knowledge and the learning process itself into component parts increases the control and predictability of the designer (teacher). Consequently the determination of learning, or what the technocratic ideologue would call either "performance indicators" or "outputs," must be seen as observable behavior. Otherwise, the particular rationality of the system would break down at the most crucial point.

A sociology of knowledge analyses of technological consciousness should be concerned with its influence on the reality constituting process the student experiences. For example, does the student learn to view experience in terms of discrete components, to view as real only what can be quantified, and to invoke the power of experts. There are also important questions relating to the reality-constituting influence of having one's experience rationally integrated with a machine-like social process. What effect, for example, does socialization have on the student when reinforcement is rationally articulated to predetermined behaviors? Does the student develop taken-for-granted attitudes about being a corporate part of a social system organized along the lines of a machine? What constitutes deviant behavior when one is part of a system that has been organized to produce in the most efficient manner predetermined products? What will be the effect of not encountering those modes of learning that cannot be organized according to the principles of purposive rationality? Will the imposition of a systems approach on certain areas of experience create absurdities that may go undetected by the limiting socialization the student is processed through? For example, the following is a behavioral objective in the arts: "Students will use appropriate vocabulary to describe art forms." The teacher is required to provide an estimate of the percentage of students in the class who will "satisfactorily achieve objective by Grade 6."

Perhaps the most important concerns, however, relate to the consequences of socializing students to a view of the culture that has been stripped of any complexity and ambiguity that would otherwise disrupt the efficiency of the system. For example, curriculum materials that contain predetermined questions and answers reduce the possibility for genuine inquiry. The use of such materials also precludes utilizing the student's phenomenological culture as an important reference point in the educational process. What the student encounters in the "packaged" curriculum is an external, objectified world that has already been organized into the proper categories; it is not a world that reflects how the individual makes choices and assigns meanings and values. The former is a world of accumulated knowledge that involves a passive stance on the part of the student; the latter involves a social-historical world that is subject to reinterpretation as students attempt to understand it in terms of their evolving existential frame of reference.

The analysis of the public school curricula is an important task in the sociology of knowledge primarily because it reveals the influence of different modes of organizing knowledge on the consciousness of the student. The working vocabulary of the sociology of knowledge (inter-subjectivity, taken for granted, reification, life world, intentionality, etc.) provides the conceptual lenses for seeing important aspects of classroom socialization that previously went largely unnoticed or were distorted by the tendency to view student learning in terms of behavior. Understanding how communication facilitates the reality constituting process of socialization carries with it a new set of implications for the educator. After the educator has made explicit the influence of the curriculum on the development of the student's conceptual maps, there is the inevitable subsequent question that must be dealt with—the question of how to improve the educational influence on the student. This question should also be seen as being in the legitimate domain of the sociology of knowledge. The concepts that help illuminate how culture is communicated and internalized as part of the student's conceptual maps can be used as the basis of a theory of curriculum reform.

NOTES

1. Gregory Bateson, *Mind and Nature* (New York: Bantam Books, 1980), 32.
2. Social Science Staff of the Educational Research Council of America, *Industry: Man and Machine* (Boston: Allyn and Bacon, 1971), 2–3.
3. Lev Semenovich Vygotsky, *Thought and Language* (Cambridge, Mass.: MIT Press, 1962), 119.
4. Basil Bernstein, *Class, Codes and Control*, vol. 3 of *Towards a Theory of Educational Transmission*, 2nd ed. (London: Routledge and Kegan Paul, 1977). See also Pierre Bourdieu and Jean Claude Passeron, *Reproduction in Education Society, and Culture* (London: Sage Publishers, 1977).
5. Len Barton, Roland Meighan, and Stephen Walker, *Schooling, Ideology and the Curriculum* (Barcombe, Lewes: Falmer Press, 1980), 186.

6. Hugh Mehan, "Social Constructionism in Psychology and Sociology," *The Quarterly Newsletter of the Laboratory of Comparative Human Cognition 3* (October 1981): 71–77.

7. Peter Berger and Stanley Pullberg, "Reification and the Sociological Critique of Consciousness," in *History and Theory*, vol. 4 (1964–1965), 196–211.

8. Peter Berger and Thomas Luckmann, *The Social Construction of Reality* (Garden City, N.Y.: Anchor Books, 1967), 89.

9. Clyde Kluckhohn, "The Gift of Tongues," in *Intercultural Communication*, ed. Larry Samover and Richard Porter (Belmont, Calif.: Wadsworth Publishers, 1972).

10. Paul Hanna, Clyde F. Kohn, John R. Lee, and Clarence L. Ver Steeg, *Investigating Man's World* (Glenview; Ill.: Scott, Foresman, 1970), 113.

11. The idea about how the legitimation process is used in the reality-sharing process was articulated by Peter Berger and Thomas Luckmann, *The Social Construction of Reality*, 92–124.

12. Michael F. D. Young, ed., *Knowledge and Control* (London: Collier-Macmillan, 1971), 38.

4

A Sociology of Knowledge
Approach
to Curriculum Development

Although there are many factors that influence the student's pattern of thought, what happens in the language environment of the classroom, nonetheless, remains fundamentally important. The connection between language and thought, which has near universal recognition in most academic circles, means that educational theorists and classroom teachers cannot be excused from understanding the role that language plays in transmitting the conceptual maps that enables students to participate in a shared social world. Even though nineteenth century positivism still dominates the thinking in most teacher-training institutions, as well as in governmental efforts to change education, the fact remains that the basic reality of the classroom is the language environment that both establishes the boundaries within which thought occurs while providing the linguistic foundations that makes thought and communication possible. Nor can we dismiss the importance of understanding the role language plays in the social construction of reality because the theory we use lacks the élan of revolutionary rhetoric that promises (though seldom leads to) fundamental transformations in society. While other theoretical frameworks may focus more explicitly on the political and economic forces that influence which groups of students have access to which bodies of school knowledge, the sociology of knowledge we have been attempting to use puts in focus the most perennial, educational relationship that occurs in all forms of societies where teachers are introducing students to new cultural territory by giving them the language and the concomitant conceptual maps for naming and thinking about "what is."

Abstract theory about attaining more just social relationships serves a purpose in fixing moral priorities within an increasingly materialistic and relativistic social context, but the basic relationship that leads incrimentally either to liberating or controlling thought occurs in the moment of primary socialization. As the history of emissary prophecy shows, as well as the more recent efforts of revolutionary educational theorists, sweeping visions have had little influence on the everyday lives of people. As many individuals have discovered, it is difficult to translate these visions into the more mundane world of experience. Understanding how the patterns of the everyday world are shared and sustained through communication, while appearing banal to the more apocalyptically-minded, can lead to changing the dynamics of the socialization process. Rather than treat the sociology of knowledge of Schutz, Berger, and Luckmann as a somewhat pedestrian event in the history of ideas, the implications of their theory for curriculum development should be explored.[1] A better understanding of the "moves" in the language game of primary socialization may enable us to see how theory can lead to an alternative practice.

The "moves" in the language game of socialization occur regardless of whether the participants are aware of them. As the participants encounter each other, bringing the conceptual maps that reflect their own social biographies, communication may lead to one of the participants playing the role of significant other. The communication may take the form of the significant other's body language serving as a message system in a previously unfamiliar social context (e.g., the body language that communicates indifference when one has lost or been wounded in a social encounter), or it may take the more conventional form of a verbal explanation that introduces an element of the social world not thought about before by the person being socialized (e.g., "Entrophy relates to culture in the following ways ...," "Modern art is ...," "That decision is made by the management!"). As the meaning is internalized, the social world that can be understood by the individual's conceptual maps is expanded. It is trite though necessary to say that not all communication leads to socialization. Often people talk at each other and due to differences in conceptual maps, intentionality, and critical thought, their respective worlds of meaning are not shared. There are also situations where communication, when characterized by conflict and disagreement, serves to maintain the participants' pre-established definitions of reality. But in the classroom where the participants share conceptual maps based on shared assumptions and categories for organizing everyday reality, communication continually involves a dependency relationship where the student is being introduced to new cultural territory. Often, it may simply be a matter of giving students the formal vocabulary and explanatory framework that serves as the conventional way to think about part of the culture they have tacitly learned to operate in at a functional level. The student can also change roles with the teacher and become the significant other who introduces the teacher to new cultural domains.

Understanding the "moves" of the language game of socialization leads to a more detached perspective on how one is involved in the communication process. If teachers are ego-involved in getting students to accept a part of the culture they experience as taken for granted, it is unlikely that the teachers will be able to exercise the reflective awareness that enables them to recognize how they control the dynamics of the socialization process. But when teachers are not ego-involved, which is always problematic (given Nietzsche's observation about how our "will to power" influences what we are capable of knowing), they can view themselves as actors playing out a culturally prescribed scenario. Knowing when an explanation needs to be followed by one that enables the student to gain a different perspective and when to take a different tack by asking "Where did we get that idea or value?" is what separates a good teacher from one who simply fetters the student's mind with taken-for-granted beliefs.

If we look at our own recent history of dealing with sexist attitudes, we can see how teachers changed the "moves" in the language game of socialization. Prior to the general awareness of sexist attitudes in our culture, teachers reinforced the taken-for-granted attitudes based on assumptions about the basic physical and intellectual inequality between the sexes. As the curriculum introduced students to new areas of the culture that involved gender distinctions, primary socialization contributed to the student's conceptual maps that created a natural attitude toward the inferiority of women. For example, the omission of women historians, artists, theologians, mathematicians, and so forth, was an important part of the public school curriculum in that students were conditioned to think that only men could perform these roles. The reproduction of conventional attitudes involved teachers and textbooks making available the language that served as an information code for thinking about gender difference. Words and sentences that named previously unthought of aspects of social reality laid down a mental grid that would guide future thought and behavior, until events and personal reflection forced the individual to question what previously was part of a natural attitude. The teacher's body language, vocabulary, and conceptual maps communicated a natural attitude toward the objective, factual nature of the culture of inequality. All the moves in the language game of socialization—naming "what is," modelling the natural attitude appropriate to the situation, establishing whether the new element of social reality was to be viewed as objectively real or as a subjective phenomena, and reproducing through the communication process the deep categories and assumptions that determine the pattern of thought—occurred simultaneously and generally below the level of conscious awareness of the participants.

The politicizing of taken-for-granted, sexist beliefs served to relativize the authority of traditional beliefs. Although we are familiar with the social events that followed, it is important to review what happened in order to see how changes in socialization led to an increased level of communicative competence. It is also important to recognize that the relativizing of taken-for-granted beliefs did not lead to social chaos and disintegration, but followed a dynamic process that we have witnessed countless times when old beliefs are discredited and replaced with a new set of taken-for-granted attitudes. As political pressure in society led to widespread examination and discussion of cultural patterns based on sexist attitudes attention became increasingly focused on the primary socialization occurring in the classroom. It was found that teachers and textbooks were engaged in reproducing in the minds of the students the conceptual maps that were being challenged in the larger political arena. As a consensus formed on the inappropriateness of socializing students to sexist attitudes, teachers began to alter the "moves" in the language game. For example, the limited vocabulary that previously served to establish in the student's mind the occupational possibilities open to men and women was expanded, with the consequence that it became possible to think of women performing in work roles that previously could not have been imagined. Instead of body language, voice intonation, and so forth, that communicated a sense of taken-for-grantedness toward traditional patterns of cultural bias, teachers communicated a taken for granted attitude toward questioning all recognized forms of sexual inequality. (Teachers by no means moved in lock step but they did move, and that is the main point!) Where previously statements about sex role differences were communicated in a manner that gave them the status of objective fact teachers were able to present students more of a perspective on the social origins of sexist practices. Some teachers were even able to make explicit the deepest cultural codes that served as the bedrock of everyday thought and behavior. In effect they became sensitive to the process of socialization itself, and even though they may not have individually heard of the sociology of knowledge they were asking questions about the processes that were strikingly similar to the questions outlined in the previous chapter.

Other examples of teachers changing the process of socialization from the tacit level to a more explicit process of examination could easily be cited. For many teachers who have resisted the current trend to transform teachers into classroom managers, the examination of cultural beliefs both sustains them intellectually and provides a modicum of justification for working in the contradictory setting of the increasingly bureaucratized school. The nature of these teachers' unique craft needs to be put in focus, particularly in these times, and strengthened by a theoretical understanding of the relationships between culture, language, and human consciousness. Metaphors like "liberating the mind," now seem strangely passé in an environment that stresses measurable objectives. But outside of the teacher-training establishment there is a growing recognition that social and ecological problems are rooted in the patterns of thought that cause people to misread the consequences of their behavior. The problem that is now being recognized was understood by Nietzsche when he said

"In *our* thought, the essential feature is fitting new material into old schemas, *making* equal what is new." In effect we are attempting to interpret the present in terms of outmoded patterns of thought. It is like trying to see into the future by looking into a rearview mirror.

The activity of the teacher, beyond managing the social relationships of the classroom, involves transmitting the symbolic culture represented in the curriculum. The uniqueness of the teacher's craft is based on an understanding that enables the teacher to recognize the educational moment and to change the normal dynamics of socialization in order to make explicit the cultural messages being communicated. The teacher's craft also involves helping the student acquire the concepts necessary for understanding and exercising critical judgment. Socialization in other social contexts seldom provides the opportunity for critical reflection. This is not to say that the sharing of taken-for-granted beliefs is equally valued by everyone. In some situations, social routines would be disrupted by making explicit the taken-for-granted beliefs on which the routines are based; questioning in these situations is often accompanied by economic and social risk. In other social settings, the sharing of taken-for-granted beliefs excludes, by virtue of the sense of naiveté of the natural attitude, other forms of awareness. But in the school setting, socialization is a more rationally organized activity that is justified on grounds that include the value of independent thought, contributing to a more socially responsible citizen, and learning to think in a manner disciplined by an awareness of the intellectual traditions of the past. High-sounding educational slogans may often disguise a desire to achieve a better social adjustment of the individual, but even though this goal is justified on the grounds of serving the individual's interests the dominant moral tradition in the West rejects forms of education that involve the deliberate indoctrination of the student. In the language of the sociology of knowledge, a form of education that involves only the learning of taken-for-granted beliefs would be viewed as morally reprehensible. This position, I believe, would be taken by both liberals and philosophic conservatives. Given this view, which distinguishes socialization in schools from the forms of socialization carried on in other social settings, the question of whether teachers understand what is unique about their craft becomes centrally important. This has become a more paramount question in recent years as educational theorists and technicians have attempted to model the process of teaching on principles derived from the areas of industrial engineering and systems thinking.

The language of "learning outcomes," "performance indicators," "behavioral objectives" are metaphors that carry the image of a student being molded and shaped by external forces. While a pretence may be maintained that this language represents a more systematic approach to thinking about traditional educational values the fact remains that the teacher's craft of transmitting the culture in a manner that encourages critical reflection is being replaced by the image of a production process that involves both the progressive de-skilling of the teacher and the manipulation of student behavior through a powerful reward system. The traditional craft of the teacher can be rescued and strengthened by understanding the connection between the content area of the curriculum and how it will be understood by the student. Understanding this connection involves recognizing the cultural pattern of thought (the *episteme*) that underlies the organization of knowledge in the curriculum unit as well as the phenomenological world of the student. The latter is essential for grasping what the student is likely to understand and how that understanding will be integrated into the student's pattern of thinking. In taking seriously the interaction between the language environment of the classroom and the student's consciousness, I am suggesting a fundamental shift away from the past, and hopefully fading, orthodoxy of dealing with observable behaviors. The tradition of phenomenology going back to Edmund Husserl, particularly the later phase of his work, enables us to talk about the student's experience in a manner that overcomes the dichotomy that separated the subjective inner world from the objective social world of facts and events.

The main concepts of this phenomenological tradition underlies the Schutz, Berger, and Luckmann interpretation of the sociology of knowledge which attempts to explain the role of communication in transmitting and sustaining the conventions of thought on which everyday life is based. But these concepts can also be used to give a new sense of understanding to what people were trying to get at when they used the word "experience." The key concepts help us to see the student's experience in terms of intentionalities that reflect choices and interpretative meanings that occur within a conceptual framework that is built up through social interaction. Thus the concept of *intentionality* points to the fact that consciousness is involved in acts of interpretation, imagination, and remembrance. The concept of *intersubjective* accounts for how language provides what Pierre Bourdieu called the "master patterns" that set the boundaries within which the individual's intentional choices and commonsense meanings will occur.[2] As the student, for example, assimilates the aspect of the master pattern or cultural schemata that organizes reality in dichotomous categories the choices, meanings, and interpretations, which reflect more of the student's existential choice, will be shaped accordingly. The concept of the intersubjective brings into focus how culture influences the existential choice of both the teacher and students. The *natural attitude* helps us recognize a mode of consciousness that encounters the world at the commonsense, non-reflective level. Understanding the student's natural attitude (or what they take for granted) becomes essential for grasping how they are experiencing the educational process. The concepts of *life world* and *multiple realities* clarify other aspects of the student's experience. The life world of the student encompasses the areas of social life that are experienced at the level of commonsense understanding. As the life world of the student is built up through social interaction, thus reflecting an element of biographical uniqueness, it is necessary to recognize that different students may be experiencing, though communicating conventional student behavior to the teacher, different realities, with the teacher's commonsense reality simply adding to the difficulty of meaningful communication.

This simplified overview of concepts derived from the phenomenological tradition is intended to challenge the notion that we can think about curriculum without recognizing that the student's conceptual maps are an important determinant of what is experienced as "meaningful." The student's consciousness is not the blank sheet (the tabula rasa) that can be programmed (to use a current metaphorical image) by the way in which the teacher organizes the curriculum. On the other hand, it is no longer adequate for the teacher to relate the content of the curriculum to the student's "experience" without understanding the connections between culture, language, and the student's natural attitude toward everyday life. Drawing upon the student's experience, as the phenomenological tradition informs us, is a far more complex and potentially powerful process than was understood in the past when educators associated learning with experience. The tradition of grounding the learning process in the student's experience, which goes back to Locke, Pestalozzi, and, more recently, Dewey, lacked an understanding of how cultural codes are internalized into consciousness and experienced by both students and teachers as the common sense world of understanding.[3] Without the insights derived from the more contemporary work in cultural linguistics, phenomenology, and the sociology of knowledge, grounding learning in the student's experience can, in too many instances, simply become a matter of reinforcing mutually-shared, taken-for-granted attitudes.

The task of thinking about curriculum in a manner that takes account of the phenomenological world of the student and the pattern of thought embedded in the culture being communicated through the curriculum appears difficult to the educator who is habituated to thinking in a dichotomous manner that neatly separates the student from the "objective knowledge" to be learned. But as one becomes familiar with a sociology of knowledge approach to thinking about the learning process it becomes relatively easy to develop a curriculum that allows students to examine the deeper levels of their cultural maps. The problem of many educators who encounter the complexity of the sociology of knowledge framework is that they acquire a few fragmentary concepts that allows them to think *about* the framework, but not enough familiarity to think *within* the framework. Thinking within the framework is both natural and exceedingly productive after one makes the transition from a dichotomous pattern of thinking to the interaction framework of dialectical thinking.

But making that transition is often difficult for classroom teachers who takes a single course that introduces them to the sociology of knowledge perspective and then takes other courses based on a fundamentally different ideology. Given this situation, our task here is to identify the principles of curriculum development that reflect a sociology-of-knowledge way of thinking and to show how these principles relate to developing the student's communicative competence.

Using the sociology of knowledge to think about curriculum leads to several basic concerns. The first relates to how the content area and pattern of thinking which underlies the organization of knowledge influences the student's conceptual map. In effect, it is a matter of asking whether the map still relates to the territory and, more importantly, whether it enables the student to read the more interesting and important features of the territory. For example, does the knowledge that is to be acquired help the student think about existential issues of choice, commitment, and meaning within the universe organized by the culture? This question leads to considering whether the curriculum helps to make explicit elements of the symbolic world created by the culture to provide answers to fundamentally human dilemmas and uncertainties. As Clifford Geertz points out, religion (ideology can also be understood as serving the same function) has traditionally provided a world view that gives emotionally convincing answers to existential questions. Stated in Geertz's more elegant style: "Religion tunes human actions to an envisaged cosmic order and projects images of cosmic order onto the plane of human existence."[4] Whether the overarching symbolic universe is referred to in terms of a religious system of beliefs, ideology, or world view or Zeitgeist is less significant than the fact that culture provides the symbolic patterns that integrate and guide thought and invests those patterns with the sense of plausibility that enables the individual to adopt a natural attitude toward the order they impose. The curriculum, whether it deals with the nature of work, time, metaphorical thinking, poverty, or ways of knowing, should be judged, in part, on the basis of whether it helps the student understand how the content area relates to the broader, overarching belief systems of the culture that influences the existential questions faced in the course of everyday life. Making the connection between the content of the curriculum and the student's life involves the identification of existential questions, and how these questions differ from the sense of wants learned from the more aggressive commercial sectors of our culture. Though the connections are more attenuated and complex than they were before the modern era, the current ways of thinking about time and work, for example, can be traced back to fundamental assumptions that served as coordinates of our world view. To introduce students to thinking about time and work, without making the connections between the deeper patterns of our belief system, as well as the existential questions faced by the students, would be to give them an inappropriate conceptual map.

The question of whether the curriculum assists students in identifying the more important features of the cultural territory can also be approached in terms of whether the curriculum enables the student to deal with the paramount political themes and issues. Just as communicative competence is essential to the possible reduction of the tension between the student's existential being and what is culturally prescribed, it is equally essential to increasing the prospects of successful survival in the social-political world. As the critical thrust of our rational process relativizes traditional patterns of authority the process of discourse becomes increasingly important to reconstituting authority on a new set of norms. What people are able to talk about, however, is influenced by many factors, including the taken-for-granted beliefs that put the socially problematic out of focus. Although the school curriculum is not the only source of the student's conceptual maps, it is nevertheless an important vehicle for providing them with the vocabulary and conceptual frameworks necessary for expressing how they think about the problems of everyday life. The content of the curriculum must, therefore, be judged on whether it provides conceptual maps that relate to social-political-ecological territory in which students will have to establish themselves as adults. If the curriculum is designed to reinforce the taken-for-granted beliefs that represent historically outmoded ways of responding to today's problems, the curriculum will serve to undermine the student's growth in communication competence.

The territory of daily life is marked by fundamental disjunctions between the dominant belief system and social-ecological conditions. The relativizing of traditional forms of authority over the last three centuries has forced the individual to operate in the intellectual and economic marketplace on the assumption that the combination of rational effort and self-interest would lead to social progress. The subsequent unleashing of human energy led to an explosion of technological development with little regard to the energy requirements for long term survival and to the evolution of a consumer-oriented culture. But the major assumptions on which this belief system was predicated did not take into account the entropic universe in which we live. While the belief system of many non-Western cultures was more closely attuned to a closed energy system that required careful conservation of resources, the dominant pattern of thinking that characterizes modern consciousness in the West is that the energy base on which the society depends is only limited by our level of technological development. The folly of this view is being increasingly recognized. But too few individuals have fully recognized the implications of the disjunction between our belief system and the phenomenon of entropy, which involves the transformation of useable energy into non-useable forms. Our culture, while operating in a closed energy system, is accelerating the use of energy sources at exponetial rates, and, therefore, is moving the entire system toward the maximum state of entropy. Pollution, as Jeremy Rifkin points out, is just one example of energy that has been transformed into an unusable state.[5]

Communicative competence could lead to the use of discourse to strengthen further the definitions of reality that support the current trajectory of the dominant culture. This can be witnessed in the manipulation of the language systems to shape consciousness for political and commercial purposes. But communicative competence can also be utilized for attempting to align our pattern of thought with the realities of the ecosystem, which seems to be the bottom line in terms of survival issues. Whether this can be done in a manner that achieves a more acceptable degree of social justice in the distribution resources and economic benefits is problematic. Though the scope of the problem far exceeds the ameliorative potential of the school, there is nevertheless a need for educators to take responsibility for insuring that the content of the curriculum provides the student with the opportunity to examine the relationship between the conceptual maps that serve as guides to everyday life and the deeper assumptions on which these maps are based.

In developing an approach to curriculum that provides an understanding of where our most basic categories and assumptions came from, the educator faces a second basic problem that is brought into focus by the sociology of knowledge perspective. The problem is created by the fact that we know more than we are aware of. The view that connects knowledge with rationality and what we can articulate does not take into account how the individual acquires a knowledge of the message systems that are necessary for survival within the culture. As a carrier of cultural knowledge, the individual can perform complex social rituals, such as changing body language as the social setting dictates, without being explicitly aware of possessing the knowledge of how to carry out the moves in that particular language game. Similarly, the individual's thoughts and emotions are organized in accordance with the acquired master patterns of the culture. Even the answers to existential questions are worked out within a conceptual framework that reflects how the culture views the human predicament.

The task facing the person who develops a curriculum is to help the student obtain the distance necessary for reflecting on the tacit forms of cultural knowledge. This process of obtaining distance from one's own taken-for-granted patterns of thinking can be carried out in a variety of ways. Paulo Freire's technique of representing visually different situations that characterize everyday life allows the individual to recognize the themes and patterns that would otherwise be hidden by the natural attitude. Studs Terkel's ability to elicit from people rich verbal accounts of their phenomenological worlds suggests the possibility of externalizing through talk worlds that would otherwise escape direct attention. Literature has been a more traditional source that enabled the individual to recognize the existential themes embedded in his or her own natural attitude.

Helping students obtain the distance from their taken-for-granted beliefs and practices can be achieved through a variety of means, but the process itself can involve a deep sense of risk. It is essential to provide the psychological support that insures the sense of trust on which dialogue is based. The psychological implications of being able to help make explicit the foundations of the individual's taken-for-granted world cannot simply be dealt with by packaging a set of techniques that are then made available to teachers. The process of rethinking elements of one's conceptual maps involves moving into liminal space where previously held positions are momentarily suspended. The reconstitution of conceptual maps, if it is going to involve the cognitive and emotional participation of the person who will have to live with the consequences of the reconstituted map, should be characterized by an open attitude toward evidence, alternative ways of thinking, as well as the possibility that significant elements of the individual's maps may be judged as worth preserving. Moving into this liminal psychological and conceptual space cannot occur if the teacher has predetermined answers and behavioral objectives built into the lesson plans, nor can it occur if teachers are unable to confront their own taken-for-granted beliefs. The psychological maturity of the teacher is an area with which most teacher-training institutions avoid getting involved, except in extreme cases. But another condition essential to the success of helping students examine taken-for-granted beliefs, that relates to the teacher's ability to decode the culture, is an area in which teacher-training institutions can take more responsibility without getting involved in the troublesome area of psychological assessment. I shall return to this issue later when I consider the policy implications of the professional education of teachers.

The growing recognition that the ideas representing our explicit knowledge (what we have used as the basis for measuring intelligence) are only a part of the knowledge of the culture is a third major problem for the curriculum developer. Our traditional view of the rational process reflects the Western bias toward viewing ideas and theory as the primary ways of representing reality. If knowledge could not be expressed in terms of explicitly articulated ideas, the individual would be judged as not being in possession of worthwhile knowledge. This bias toward ideas and theory, particularly in their more abstract forms, is reflected in the ideological traditions of Western liberalism and Marxism. Both treat the language of liberation as though it were free of all cultural orientations. This bias is also reflected in the work of technologists who create systems and models that do not take account of the cultural context in which they are to be used. We have only been able to maintain this bias toward explicit forms of knowledge by ignoring the foundations, rooted deeply in the language systems of the culture, that are largely hidden from view. If we acknowledge the tacit forms of knowledge that constitute the individual's phenomenological culture, we might recognize more readily the complex foundation of cultural knowledge which remains largely hidden when we view the visible part of the structure (explicit knowledge) as the main part of the edifice.[6] The ability of the average individual to interact successfully with a complex array of technology without being able to articulate an understanding of the difference between social and mechanical technology, or the pattern of thinking that is built into our technology, is one of many examples of the tacit forms of knowledge. Speaking a language, while taking into account the rules that govern body language and code switching dictated by different social contexts, is another example of possessing a form of knowledge that does not fit the traditional view of explicit forms of understanding.

The dominant view in education seems to have followed the traditional bias in philosophy that recognized only explicit forms of knowledge; as a consequence, we have little understanding of how tacit knowledge is acquired and how we use it to maintain the patterns of daily life. The movement within educational circles to make the student's observable behavior the only criterion for determining teacher effectiveness (references to what the student "learns," "understands," and "comprehends" are being challenged on the grounds that these terms are too ambiguous) reflects the extreme position. The emphasis on breaking concepts, skills, and activities into component parts that can be systematically presented, along with a highly rationalized reward schedule, ignores the unintended teaching that Jules Henry referred to as the "noise" in the communicative process that accompanies what is taught at the explicit level (i.e., all the cultural orientations, values, and patterns that are learned at the tacit level).[7] In the language of the sociology of knowledge, Henry was identifying how the teacher's natural attitude permeated every phase of classroom activity and was internalized by students as the natural attitude toward the world of the classroom. The teaching of history involves, for example, transmitting to the students as part of the "noise" or tacit knowledge the cultural pattern for organizing our sense of time and progress. Teaching art generally involves tacit cultural messages that lead the student to think of creativity as primarily an individual act rather than to see the hidden influence of the culture. Other examples of how explicit forms of knowledge can only be transmitted within tacit master patterns that establish a congruence between the grammar of individual thought and that of the culture are too numerous to cite.

In thinking about the forms of curriculum and pedagogy intended to contribute to the student's communicative competence, it is important to recognize that the student, even in the early grades, is a carrier of a complex array of tacit knowledge and that the organization of knowledge in the curriculum, as well as the process of teaching itself, involves the sharing of tacit understandings as to how to organize reality. The recognition of the complexity of the students' cultural maps helps to overcome the occupational hazzard of making judgments about the students' intelligence when their pattern of thought does not coincide with the pattern of thinking used in the classroom. Recognizing the students' tacit knowledge of culture is also important in terms of curriculum development and the process of teaching itself. This involves something more than simply relating content and teacher talk to the students' experience, a practice that is now commonsense among classroom practitioners. While the metaphor of "experience" refers to the subjective world of the student, the nature of tacit knowledge is such that it is not likely to be part of what the student is aware of and thus he or she cannot communicate it to the teacher. Although it is part of the students' natural attitudes, tacit knowledge influences behavior at a sub-conscious level of awareness. It includes, as pointed out earlier, the schemas or master patterns transmitted through language for organizing our sense of reality. Like the cultural rules that govern eye contact, body language, and metaphorical thinking, this tacit knowledge reproduces the deeper structures that underlie the students' experience. But the student, like the fish who was unable to discover water, will generally be unable to recognize the cultural rules that dictate so much of thought and behavior. The experience of the student is a limited educational resource as long as the teacher fails to recognize that what the student takes for granted about experience will remain beyond the scope of awareness and thus beyond the range of reflection. In a sense, the art of the teacher is in recognizing the cultural codes that are embedded in what students communicate about their experiences. It also involves recognizing that the knowledge being shared with students reproduces the tacit structures of thought.

When socialization of students to the dominant belief system is limited to reading a textbook and listening to a teacher talk, there is a danger of oversimplification and ideal-type representation of the social world. There is also the possibility that students will be unable to relate the symbolic knowledge to their own world. Hearing or reading about the social world may leave the student dependent on words for understanding other words. Socialization that corresponds to what Freire called the banking model can lead to building up explanatory frameworks that conflict with what the student encounters in the "real world." The grade school student, for example, who learns about the virtue of individualistic pioneers and about individualism as an ideal-type that leads to success in artistic creation, work, and social life acquires an important part of an explanatory framework that often does not hold up in real life in which individualism may lead to being shunned, feared, and mocked. This example, one that could be duplicated in terms of what is taught about the nature of work, success, social progress, as well as many other fundamental coordinates of our conceptual maps, suggests the possibility of a symbolic world increasingly removed from the context of everyday life. This leads to a kind of symbolic schizophrenia where the world of thought operates at a different level from the tacit knowledge necessary for social survival. It is similar to the person who learns at the tacit level to manage the behaviors socially required of the aged, but carries as part of the conceptual baggage a map that represents aging as a debilitating condition. The person may continue to manage successfully a complex set of social relationships but still feel the sense of inadequacy dictated by the culturally prescribed way of thinking.

The curriculum can introduce students to the best of their cultural heritage as well as provide the opportunity to examine the taken-for-granted beliefs and practices of the adult world. At the same time the curriculum should be organized in a manner that incorporates the themes and patterns of thought that characterizes the students' phenomenological world.The sociology of knowledge provides the concepts for making the connection between the more traditional content of the curriculum, which provides exposure to the cultural heritage, and the phenomenological culture of the student. As suggested in an earlier work, *Cultural Literacy for Freedom*,[8] the sociology of knowledge not only explains how taken-for-granted beliefs are shared, but also suggests alternative moves in the language game that can be viewed as principles for guiding thinking about curriculum development. These principles relate to the problem of obtaining distance from the taken-for-granted beliefs and conceptual categories that constitute the students' mental maps. After the teacher has identified the topic or theme of the curriculum, there is the problem of relating the abstract forms of knowledge communicated through talk and reading to the students' phenomenological world. The focus of the curricuulum unit could, for example, be on the nature of metaphorical thinking. The same principles of curriculum organization could be applied to teaching about technology, work, competition, and so forth.

FIRST PRINCIPLE: UTILIZING STUDENTS' PHENOMENOLOGICAL CULTURE

The first principle is to incorporate the students' phenomenological culture (those dimensions of the students' life world pertinant to the curriculum topic) into the process of socialization. Relating classroom discussion to the students' experience is already a traditional practice of many teachers. Involving the students' phenomenological world, however, goes beyond engaging students in a discussion of how their experience leads them to think about the issues under discussion. As mentioned earlier, the pattern of organizing thoughts and feelings, as well as those elements of the students' conceptual map experienced as the natural attitude toward everyday life, will influence what (and how) the student will contribute to the discussion, but will generally remain beyond the scope of student awareness. If the teacher understands how the phenomenological world of the student is constituted, it is then possible to make explicit important elements of the students' tacit knowledge.

In introducing students to the nature of metaphorical thinking, the teacher can start either with a formal explanation or with examples derived from the student's own language environment. If the starting point is the student's own language environment, the teacher will be operating in the student's phenomenological territory and must be sensitive to what the student is not likely to be aware of. The metaphors might include examples of student dress, car embellishments, peer-group jargon (airhead, nerd, spaced out, etc.), and the metaphorical language that characterizes the subjects they study: physical education (game plan, competition, win, good sport), social studies (democracy, change, power, freedom, equality), science (bond, inert, starfish, wave, energy, matter, atom), art (visual metaphors relating to architecture, dress, layout of space, as well as the verbal language of creativity, modern, contemporary). The collecting of evidence from the student's language environment will undoubtedly yield different and rich examples of metaphorical thinking. By starting with the student's phenomenological world, the teacher has a better guide for aiming the discussion at a level at which the student can relate verbal abstractions to the concreteness of his or her own life world. This approach also communicates an important message to the student about the purpose of the learning process: By taking the student's phenomenological world seriously the teacher is saying, in effect, that the student's culture deserves serious attention. This is a fundamentally different message than is communicated when the teacher ignores the student's culture and proceeds to dispense the new culture that is supposed to confer respectability and success.

If the teacher were to ask the students to keep a record of the different metaphors they use as they move from one area of their language environment to another, the teacher might encounter the initial blank stares. This response is an indicator of how unaware we are of the structure and content of what is termed experience. But encouragement, as well as some coaching of what to look for, will lead students to identify numerous examples that can then be integrated into the more theoretical and abstract considerations of what metaphorical thinking involves. Giving students the language for naming different aspects of their phenomenological world enables them to be aware of what previously existed as part of their tacit knowledge. One example of this phenomena occurred when we incorporated into our language a vocabulary that named sexist behavior. Suddenly, what had been an invisible aspect of our life world became the focus of awareness. Getting students to be aware of metaphorical thinking, or how they experience other aspects of culture, is also a matter of naming and providing theoretical frameworks.

Unlike the example of metaphorical thinking, the curriculum may cover topics and themes unrelated to the phenomenological world of the student. In some instances, the student's learning will be necessarily dependent on written accounts and the teacher's explanations about how to think. But there are many topics and themes that can be enriched by utilizing the phenomenological world of members in the community. The differences between reading about work or competition in the abstract and listening to a person give a description of what they are experiencing in a particular social situation is fundamental. Although the criticism may be made that the individual's experience is subjective and thus serves as an inadequate basis for generalizations, the analytical tools made available by the theorists of phenomenology enable us to recognize that the recounting of experience reveals the master conceptual patterns that are shared within the culture to organize experience; recounting also reveals the tension between the intentionality of the subject and the taken-for-granted beliefs that reflect the unconscious process of socialization. The description, if given in an atmosphere that encourages candor rather than telling the listeners what one wants to hear, will reveal the complex texture of the life world. As a reference point, the phenomenological description provides a more human dimension to the process of socialization than what often exists when the student encounters written or verbal accounts that are disconnected from experience. The phenomenological account of working at a particular task, of being a member of a minority group. of dreaming about what the future holds, of dealing with everyday life in suburbia or the city, changes the scope of socialization, and thus the student's conceptual horizon.

The Foxfire curriculum on folk traditions and the oral history approach that has become increasingly popular serve as examples of how to utilize the community as a curriculum resource. We can also see in the collected interviews of Studs Terkel the more complex view that is revealed when we take seriously what people have to say about their own lives. People who may be reduced in textbooks to an occupational category or a statistic come alive in a manner that reveals the complex mixture of intelligent understanding of personal situations, the shaping forces of culture, and the areas of existential silence. The community contains the same cross section of cultural experience that Terkel captures in *Working* and *American Dreams: Lost and Found*. The experience of caring for the health of others, of cleaning up after people, of working at a desk, of being rich, of being poor, of being old, and so on, can be incorporated into the curriculum if the teacher recognizes that the culture to which the students are being socialized is part of the life world of the members of the community. Incorporating the phenomenological dimension of culture is not meant as a substitute for the perspective that is gained through reading books, listening to the teacher's description, and viewing film; it is meant as an essential supplement.

SECOND PRINCIPLE: USE OF HISTORICAL PERSPECTIVE TO DEOBJECTIFY KNOWLEDGE

The sociology of knowledge explanation of how the use of language often leads to objectifying what is being communicated points to a second principle that must be incorporated into the development of a curriculum. The objectification process involves, as previously pointed out, losing sight of the human authorship of what is being communicated. Written and verbal statements appear to represent an objective state of affairs. That these statements were made by individuals possessing conceptual frameworks that influence how they view and interpret the world, tends not to be recognized. For the student, particularly when reading, language appears to communicate a world that is objectively real and thus factual. Some students, of course, are able to check what they read and hear against their own stock of knowledge and are able to recognize that what is being communicated to them represents someone else's interpretation. But for a great number of students, including the more sophisticated, the constant mystification of human authorship remains a problem that affects the student's sense of agency and thus his or her communicative competence. When the student encounters, during primary socialization, interpretations of the author that are represented as an objective statement of fact, the student will generally lack the conceptual means to question. This is what primary socialization means, being dependent on a significant other to name "what is." As students internalize into their conceptual framework the "factual" information about a new area of the social world. This misrepresentation will shape their own way of viewing what aspects of the social world should be reinterpreted. Their communicative competence may be limited to naming and defending, for reasons having to do with ego involvement in one's conceptual maps, the "factual" knowledge they possess.

A typical example of how human authorship is mystified in textbooks is the following statement of "fact."

> One of the most thrilling and exciting experiences in your lifetime is to secure and start work on your first full-time job. The transition from school to work is more than finding a job. It is obtaining a freedom from dependence on your parents. . . . You must join other consumers and use your earnings to achieve the most happiness for yourself and those you care about. . . . Programs on radio and television have been designed to assist consumers in getting the most for their money.[9]

Since this example appears in a high school textbook, it is not likely to be part of the primary socialization of most students, though a case could be made that it may serve to reinforce a part of the cultural map that students may have acquired at an earlier stage of socialization. The quotation is reproduced here primarily for the purpose of demonstrating how an author's cultural orientation is transformed through the medium of language into an objective picture of the world. Even more reflective authors and speakers face the same problem. What they say and write has a way of being objectified and taking on a life of its own. Language becomes the index of what is real, and the author often ceases to be part of the picture.

In organizing the curriculum, the teacher needs to keep the problem of objectified knowledge clearly in focus. This is often difficult because much of the teacher's socialization will have been based on "objective knowledge," and will be likely a part of the teacher's taken-for-granted beliefs. The consequence is that the part of the teacher's stock of knowledge that is taken for granted will continue to be part of the tacit socialization that escapes critical scrutiny (although it escapes scrutiny it may not be accepted by students with a different frame of reference). It should also be added that not all of the teacher's "factual knowledge" that buttresses the taken-for-granted world is wrong or dysfunctional. Nonetheless an awareness of the process of objectification, as well as its consequences for students, should be part of the teacher's craft.

The language that socializes students by expanding their conceptual maps can be deobjectified by providing a historical perspective. If students can only hear references to the "state," "freedom," "individualism," "progress," and so forth, without understanding that the metaphors reproduce elements of the cultural maps that characterize the period from which they were derived, they may relate to the terms as though they refer to objective conditions. Providing a historical perspective, whether it is a part of the curriculum dealing with the metaphorical nature of language (a topic that is so broad that it underlies most areas of the curriculum) or dealing with the nature of work, or literary forms, is essential to giving students the sense that the social-cultural world has human authorship. The awareness that beliefs, institutions, and social practices do not have a unique ontological status that establishes their truth claims beyond the relativizing influence of history and culture alters the student's relationship to the authority of what is being learned. Objectified knowledge centers authority in itself and makes questioning more difficult. Primary socialization, that involves explanations about the historical development of ideas, institutions, and social practices, shifts authority to the individual who is attempting to understand.

Integrating a historical perspective into whatever is being studied alters the reality constituting process of primary socialization in another fundamental way. A key feature of our current Western cultural map is that the individual is at the center of the stage. Some might even argue that in many instances the sense of individualism, expressed in terms of self-realization and self-expression, leads individuals to act as though they were the only actors on the stage. A convincing argument could even be made that this view of self-formed, self-governing indivdualism reflects a process of primary socialization to an objectified world of things, facts, and values that exist, as in a supermarket, as so many choices available to the individual. However, this is a false form of individual authority. The historical perspective adds to the individual's way of understanding the dimension of social memory which Hannah Arendt saw as essential to establishing authority on a critical, reflective basis. Awareness of how things were in the past and their continuity in the present, alters the view that we are self-formed and self-governing individuals. In this way, students might recognize more fully the tension between proposed changes and the continuity that connects their life world to the past and also that the tensions call for a careful consideration of what aspects of the past should be permanently severed.

The historical dimension also relates to the individual's communicative competence. If there is an awareness of how the social-cultural world evolved, the individual will possess, by virtue of this understanding, not only the dimension of memory but also the language essential for negotiating with individuals and institutions that attempt to control social experience by manipulating thought. An example relates to the increasing emphasis in "rationalizing" the work process in order to increase "efficiency." If the person's conceptual map does not include socialization to how the worker in the past exercised control over the work still itself, it would be difficult for the person to challenge the incorporation into the work place of the values of efficiency and rationalization that are among the higher values of our cultural period. Access to the social dimension of memory provides the perspective for holding people accountable for ensuring that changes represent a genuine improvement in the human condition. The progressive de-skilling of the worker is not something that can be easily negotiated when essential aspects of our collective maps fuse rationalization and efficiency with progress.

The historical perspective can be added to the socialization process at all stages of the educational process, from the earliest grades where students are introduced to the most basic coordinates of our conceptual maps to the graduate level where the reified categories used to organize academic knowledge are transmitted through the primary socialization process. If students learn to "tell" time, and to view it as passing in a manner that is quite independent of the individual, they are acquiring a conceptual map that is quite different from the one they would have if they understood the historical (and cultural) origins of our mechanical view of time. Similarly, the graduate student who understands the ideological roots of positivism might recognize more fully the strengths and weaknesses of empirical research. But adding the historical perspective to the socialization process points to a policy issue that is central to the education of teachers. At one level it is being suggested that adding the historical dimension is an alternative move in the language game that teachers control. In this sense, adding a historical dimension might be viewed as a technique that can be learned along with all the other technique and strategies that are viewed as an essential parts of the teacher's professional knowledge. But at another level, translating this more reflexive form of socialization into another technique for effective classroom management would be a perversion. In order to add the historical dimension that teacher has to possess a historical knowledge of the subject he or she is teaching. Without this essential element the teacher will be limited to sharing with the student his or her own taken-for-granted, objectified knowledge, or interpreting to the students the information given in the textbook. The policy issue, to state it more directly, relates to whether the segregation of teaching strategies into separate professional courses is as effective as learning a field of knowledge and then extrapolating the dynamics of the socialization process (teaching strategies) in a manner that mediates between the unique characteristics of the field of knowledge and the life world of the student. The latter view, if seen as a wise policy for the education of teachers, would lead to a closer relationship between the academic and professional education of teachers.

THIRD PRINCIPLE: INCORPORATING A CROSS-CULTURAL PERSPECTIVE

A third principle that should guide curriculum development involves incorporating whenever possible a cross-cultural perspective. If we return to the image of the teacher-student relationship as a language game, it is possible to recall that one of the most critical "moves" involved transmitting, along with the explicit information that the teacher wants to get across, the deep codes that represent the cultural patterns for organizing thought. The deep code (or what Pierre Bourdieu called the "master patterns") reproduces the episteme of the culture; while it serves the vital function of transmitting assumptions and categories that make up the conceptual grammar used to organize thought, the deep code itself is seldom made explicit. Except in those situations involving a fundamental re-thinking of the assumptions underlying everyday activities, like in the re-thinking of the Newtonian world view (not exactly an example of everyday experience) or the penetrating examination of our most fundamental assumptions about the progressive nature of technology, the deep codes usually are shared tacitly through primary socialization and continually reinforced through conversation. These codes represent the hidden patterns of our way of understanding. Even though the most basic assumptions and categories may undergo change, like in the shift from a self-denial to a remissive view of individualism, deep codes are seldom made explicit in the process of socialization. Like the conceptual pattern that causes a person in our culture to think in categories that separate reality neatly into true and false, right and wrong, or to think of time as linear and progressive, the deep conceptual codes serve as a conceptual lens that bring into focus certain aspects of the world, while blurring other aspects. But the lenses that help us bring the world into focus, the codes themselves, are generally not seen.

Incorporating a cross-cultural perspective into the curriculum unit helps to overcome the difficulty of recognizing the conceptual categories and assumptions that underlie the students' taken-for-granted beliefs. The phenomenological description enables students to externalize and obtain distance from the culture they otherwise would experience as the natural attitude toward everyday life. The cross-cultural comparison further enables students to obtain the necessary perspective for recognizing the deep codes on which the natural attitude is based. If students are examining the nature of work, technology, individualism, modernization, or competition—to cite just a few of the possible themes of the curriculum— studying how the deep categories and assumptions of another culture lead to differences in taken-for-granted beliefs would help students recognize the cultural underpinnings of their own natural attitudes. Simply talking to students about the deep codes that influence how they think and experience the everyday world will most often be met with incomprehension, since socialization leaves most people with the belief that their experience represents an objective state of reality. That experience and thought are based on a particular set of cultural codes is generally not part of the message communicated through primary socialization.

Cross-cultural comparisons introduce students to another insight of the sociology of knowledge, namely that there are multiple realities. Understanding the dangers of generalizing that other people experience the same natural attitudes seems particularly relevant in today's world where interacting with people of other cultures becomes, for many people, a common occurence. This understanding will not lead to immediate answers of how to resolve the problems that arise when people with different cultural codes interact, but it should contribute to overcoming the extreme naivety that is reflected in the tendency to assume that other people share the same world view. This naivety is particularly prevalent in the assumptions that surround the export of our form of technology and political ideology to Third World countries. The argument that the awareness of the reality constructs of other cultures involves the relativizing of the students' belief system will undoubtedly be raised. People who are likely to raise this objection often assume that the relativizing process leads to anomic forms of individualism, and thus weakens the commitment to shared values and understandings. Since this question shall be discussed in the conclusion of this book, it will suffice at this time to point out that the core beliefs of Western thought (power of rational thought, individualism, the progressive nature of change, and the secular universe) contribute in a far more powerful way to relativizing the hold that traditional cultural values have on individual consciousness. But these values have been reproduced from generation to generation, often in our most prestigious schools, in a manner that hid both their relativizing influence on traditional cultural values and their culturally specific nature. A more reflexive approach to socialization simply represents a more honest stance for the teacher to take; it is also a more useful approach in terms of contributing to the students' communicative competence.

Thinking of curriculum development in terms of a sociology of knowledge, understanding of the "reality constituting" nature of communication in the classroom does not necessarily mean that a totally new approach must be taken and that existing textbooks and materials have to be abandoned. Although it would be desirable in some instances to develop new curriculum materials that bring into focus the interplay between the deep codes that shape the pattern of thinking and everyday experience, the teacher can often begin to engage students in a more reflexive form of socialization by using textbooks and materials as representative of the taken-for-granted beliefs that need to be made explicit. The textbook type description, in many ways, represents a consensus on how to think about various aspects of the culture. The teacher can present the textbook descriptions as views that are taken for granted by many people and then expand the socialization process by introducing into the discussion the phenomenological ("How does the worker experience a particular form of work?" "What is the experience of being unemployed?" "How does one experience living in a particular type of building?"), as well as the historical and cross-cultural dimensions. Checking textbook explanations against the phenomenological world of people whose social context will vary introduces the student to a more complex and realistic view; it also leads to an expanded way of thinking and talking about that area of social experience. This is essential for developing the students' communicative competence, which rests ultimately upon the student possessing the language tools for formulating thoughts and communicating them to others in a convincing manner. Socialization that involves a historical dimension *"Where did the idea or practice come from?" "What was the belief system that prevailed when the idea or practice emerged?"* will help the student to recognize the danger of making simple categorical judgments about either rejecting the past in favor of the new, or of slavish acceptance of tradition. Adding the historical dimension to the socialization process ensures a radical educational experience where the student is invited to consider root questions concerning origins, assumptions, and current relevance. Like the cross-cultural perspective, a historical understanding helps to problematize the natural attitude that limits the student's power to develop a rational defense of those elements of the culture that need preserving as well as a rational argument for reconceptualizing those aspects of an inherited belief system that no longer can be justified.

In the most fundamental sense teachers do not have a choice about whether they want to get involved in the language game called "socialization." Communicating the culture at the abstract level of words and theory is the basic tool of their trade. The real question relates to whether they carry on the socialization process in a linguistically limited manner in which students learn a vocabulary and learn tacitly shared conceptual frameworks that reproduce in consciousness the taken-for-granted beliefs of the teacher and textbook writer. The alternative (and it is not always an either-or situation) is to expand and deepen the socialization process by varying the moves in the language game that are essentially under the control of the teacher. The variations can take an infinite number of form depending on the intellectual and experiential background of both teachers and students, but teachers will be more effective in altering the moves in the language game when they understand how the acquisition of culture can both constrain and expand thought. In effect, teachers must be able to think about pedagogy and curriculum development within the conceptual framework of the sociology of knowledge.

NOTES

1. Typical examples of how Marxists view the ideas of Schutz, Berger, and Luckmann can be seen in Michael Apple, "Ideology, Reproduction, and Educational Reform," *Comparative Education Review 22* (October 1978): 359. Also see Peter Hamilton, *Knowledge and Social Structure* (London: Routledge and Kegan Paul, 1974).
2. Pierre Bourdieu, "Systems of Education and Systems of Thought," in *Knowledge and Control*, ed. Michael F. D. Young (London: Collier-Macmillan, 1971), 191–192.
3. For a view that contrasts with Dewey's understanding of the connection between language and thought, see Tracy B. Strong, "Language and Nihilism: Nietzsche's Critique of Epistemology," *Theory and Society 3* (Summer 1976), 239–261.
4. Clifford Geertz, *The Interpretation of Cultures* (New York: Basic Books), 90.
5. Jeremy Rifkin, *Entropy: A New World View* (New York: Bantam Books, 1980), 35.
6. Michael Polanyi, *The Tacit Dimension* (New York: Anchor Books, 1967). The chapter on "Tacit Knowing" is the most pertinent.
7. Jules Henry, *Culture against Man* (New York: Vintage Books, 1963), 290.
8. C. A Bowers, *Cultural Literacy for Freedom* (Eugene, Oreg.: Elan Publishers, 1974).
9. Grady Kimbrell and Ben S. Vinegrad, *Succeeding in the World of Work* (Bloomington, Ill.: McKnight & McKnight, 1970), 151.

5

Conclusion

Different pedagogical styles are based on reality sets that involve specific assumptions about power, what constitutes knowledge, and how knowledge is acquired. Yet, what is common to all pedagogies is the central role given to communication. Regardless of whether we use Freire's liberation pedagogy, the more rationalized banking approach of the behavior modifier, the exemplar model of the Zen master, or the typical classroom teacher whose practice is shaped more by a pragmatic approach to experience than by theory or an explicit epistemological position, the communication process that binds the teacher and students together involves the "reality sharing" process of socialization. Ignoring the theory that helps to explain the dynamics of the reality-sharing and maintenance process will not allow the teacher to escape either from being involved in the process, or from the responsibility of a dependency relationship. What has been attempted in the previous chapters is the elaboration of a theoretical framework that illuminates in considerable detail the basic "moves" in the language game of socialization. This was done on the assumption that understanding the nature and consequences of the different "moves" in the language game would enable the teacher to contribute to the student's communicative competence. This assumption may be as naive as Freire's assumption about the dialogical relationship of teacher and students transcending the problem of cultural invasion, but Freire's commitment, which is shaped by the economic and political realities of the Third World, seems to be the only defensible position to take. Even though the student's growth in communicative competence can be justified in terms of the increasing politicization of traditional cultural norms and sources of authority, one must recognize that increased knowledge can also be used by people who possess a different ideological framework for controlling the thoughts of other people. That progress in understanding can be used for socially undesirable, even life threatening purposes, is one of the fundamental paradoxes of the modern world. However, there seems to be no viable alternative to making the effort, even when one recognizes both the scale of apathy and the potential for distortion.

Since this is not my first attempt to use a sociology of knowledge framework to explain some of the more hidden aspects of the educational (socialization) process, as well as to suggest concrete proposals for curriculum development, I have learned to anticipate the arguments that will be raised. Some arguments must be taken seriously, while others reflect a misunderstanding of the primacy of the socialization process. Resistance often arises simply from a sense of vulnerability that accompanies the attempt to think within a new and unfamiliar framework. Therefore, I would like to identify four lines of argument that are likely to be developed by critics and then finish up with a few remarks about the reform of teacher education.

The arguments against using a sociology of knowledge framework as the primary basis for a theory of education are likely to reflect a concern about the problems of relativism, social inequality, the limited ability of teachers, and the intolerance of the community. Each of the arguments deserves fuller treatment than can be given here, but it is only possible to outline the essentials of each position and to articulate a brief response.

THE PROBLEM OF RELATIVISM

The first and perhaps most significant argument against grounding a theory of education in a sociology of knowledge framework is based on the idea that the sociology of knowledge contributes to a way of thinking that further relativizes the foundations of our values and beliefs. Those who make this argument can point to what has been upheld as one of the more important contributions of the sociology of knowledge, namely the explanation of ideas and values as expressions of social conditions. Recognizing the human authorship of the symbol systems on which the cultural patterns are based, which can lead both to the position of cultural relativism as well as to the more extreme form of subjective relativism, seemed at one time as a progressive step in the development of human understanding and tolerance. But the critics pointed out that the pattern of thought that enables people to relativize all ideas and values in the name of a higher intellectual calling, also threatens to undermine the values on which this intellectual process rests.[1] In effect the sociology of knowledge perspective must itself be seen as relative to a particular historical period of thought. At the level of the individual, according to these critics, the relativizing process erodes the civilizing conventions that have evolved over centuries, leaving the individual in a nihilistic state of mind where nothing has a compelling sense of meaning. The possession of objective knowledge as well as the authority of cultural conventions are thus replaced by extreme forms of subjective thought and behavior.

This extreme condition of existential nihilism has been explored by such writers as Dostoevski, Nietzsche, and Kafka. It has also occupied the attention of sociologists who have attempted to understand the problematic aspects of modernization. Our concern here is not with the elaboration of their arguments, which are varied and complex, but with bringing into focus the relationship between the approach to education suggested in the preceding chapters and the basic problem of relativism.

The first point to be emphasized is that the relativizing of cultural values, which is perceived as leading to the nihilist belief that existence is nothing more than our interpretation of it, is not limited to the sociology of knowledge. Though this theory may contribute to the relativizing tendencies there are other aspects of modern consciousness that erode the authority of cultural traditions. The values of freedom and equality (central to the neoromantic educators), the belief that society can free itself through revolutionary action from the authority of the past (a basic assumption of the neo-Marxist educators), the view that reason is the chief means of efficient control (the technocratic educators' panacea for achieving order and predictability), and the anthropocentric view of the universe which makes subjectivity the fulcrum of reality, all contribute to de-legitimating sources of authority that have traditionally existed outside the individual. These values, when made into absolutes, have been used to maximize individual freedom and self-expression; but the success of emancipating the individual from all forms of cultural control places on the individual a sense of responsibility that may be impossible to sustain over the long run. Like the idea of continual revolution, the burden of continually giving meaning and assuming personal responsibility may represent the modern propensity to experiment with abstract ideas without considering how culture, with its system of "commands and options," enables its members to face the existential questions within a more circumscribed horizen of responsibility.

This value orientation, which underlies the revolutionary ethos of the last two centuries, as well as the growing cult of therapeutic psychology, suggests that the sociology of knowledge represents a late arrival on the scene. Contrary to the more general acceptance of these other values, the sociology of knowledge has influenced a much smaller and more theoretically-oriented audience.

The educational use of the sociology of knowledge contributes to the relativizing process that characterizes modern thought only insofar as this approach leads students to understand the social and historical origins of their beliefs. But this dereification of cultural belief does not lead to the brink of nihilism, which is a criticism that more appropriately applies to the modernizing ideology that makes self-realization and expression the ultimate value. The pedagogical application of the sociology of knowledge introduces a social and historical perspective that enables the individual to recognize cultural continuities and to face the difficult question of how to reconcile the desire for change with the need to conserve those aspects of the past that are worth preserving. In addition, the knowledge that comes from a sociology of knowledge approach to the organization of curriculum represents more accurately the complexity of culture, and helps to foster a dialectical relationship between the individual's own groundedness in cultural tradition and the capacity to envisage new social arrangements. When one of the chief messages communicated through socialization makes ignorance of the past an educational virtue, assuming it to be a form of recovering man's lost innocence, the individual is left without the language necessary for articulating the fallacies of the anthropocentric universe, which represents the ultimate reification of modern consciousness. This scenario, rather than the one associated with the sociology of knowledge. leads to the remissive form of individualism that has few defenses against the appeal of nihilism.[2]

Although the problem of nihilism is an increasingly important aspect of modern consciousness it seems to be a source of concern primarily for intellectuals. If we look at the hold that culture exerts over our patterns of thought and behavior, we can see another set of issues that can only be dealt with by relativizing the dominant conceptual maps that influence how we view the environment. The sociology of knowledge framework helps us to recognize the strength of culture in shaping the natural attitude toward everyday life; this recognition does not negate the problem of nihilism, it simply displaces it as the only serious problem we face. If we concern ourselves with the increasing seriousness of intercultural politics and the ecological crisis, which seem both to be interrelated and the most paramount problem we face, the sociology of knowledge takes on added significance in terms of its power to illuminate the educational challenge that characterizes this point in our history. Given the fact that important elements of the conceptual maps being shared with students no longer make sense in terms of our current understanding of the ecological crisis, the belief systems of other cultures and the advances of scientific knowledge, the basic educational problem becomes one of challenging the natural attitude that is based on outmoded ways of thinking. The codifications of culture that shape our moral concerns, our strategies of defense and technological development, and our way of organizing and rewarding work, have on objective dimension to them that cannot be understood or dealt with in terms of the relativism of individual subjectivity. An approach to education that enables the student to obtain distance from the natural attitude based on these historically rooted cultural codifications contributes both to the student's ability to make choices on the basis of more explicit forms of knowleoge and to acquire the more complex language facility necessary for participating in the political process. That the sociology of knowledge provides the teacher with a way of understanding how to make explicit more of the socialization process seems to outweigh the argument that this framework promotes a relativizing perspective.

THE PROBLEM OF SOCIAL INEQUALITY AND SOCIAL REFORM

A second group of potential critics includes the neo-Marxist educators who used the sociology of knowledge of Schutz, Berger, and Luckmann as only a prelude for their more intensive engagement with the ideas of Marx. Geoff Whitty summarized the attitude of a number of educational theorists who were beginning to explore the politics of school knowledge by asserting that "the overemphasis on the notion that reality is socially constructed seems to have led to a neglect of the consideration of how and why reality comes to be constructed in particular ways and how and why particular constructions seem to have the power to resist subversion."[3] Instead of exploring the educational implications of both lines of thought, the Schutz-Berger-Luckmann stream of the sociology of knowledge as well as the Marxist stream, the neo-Marxist educational theorists chose the latter as the appropriate framework for understanding the relationship of schooling to social classes and for developing an educational theory that would be consistent with Marx's vision of a classless society. The neo-Marxists educational theorists have added to our understanding of how the selection and organization of school knowledge reproduces social class relationships (though the interpretation of this relationship tends to be more determanistic than some neo-Marxists are willing to accept), but they have been far less successful in developing a theory of education suitable for either facilitating revolutionary change or maintaining the egalitarian form of society that is to follow the revolution.

Had they continued to take seriously the Schutz-Berger-Luckmann stream of the sociology of knowledge the neo-Marxists educators might have been able to avoid making educational recommendations that were embarrassingly similar to the neoromantic position that schools (if they must exist) should facilitate the learner's freedom to define his or her own goals. As Kevin Harris stated, the problem facing educators is that: "if learning and gaining knowledge were geared to peoples' actual existential needs and interest it is difficult to see why power would be necessary at all."[4] Later in the same book, *Education and Knowledge*, Harris is led to rhapsodize about a society where education no longer serves the state in maintaining class divisions, where people "are talking, acting and working informally among themselves; discussing their lives, their freedoms, their constraints, their situations, their visions and their knowledge of the world; discovering the world for themselves through experience."[5] The essence of Harris' view of education is reflected in the prescriptive writings of other neo-Marxist educators who saw themselves as critics of the neoromantic educators. For example, Samuel Bowles and Herbert Gintis proposed that a revolutionary form of education should promote personal growth, equal and cooperative relationships, and the students' capacities to control the conditions of their lives.[6] The theme of individual emancipation is carried further by Henry Giroux who states that

> the moment of truth for a radical theory of schooling rests, on the one hand, with its ability to help students move critically within their own subjectivity and to break with the 'commonsense' assumptions that tie them to the dominant structures of power and control. . . . On the other hand the viability of such a theory also depends on its success in fostering the subjective preconditions necessary for a movement of liberation aimed at restructuring and reshaping the basic structure of society.[7]

Similar views are central to the liberation pedagogy of Paulo Freire. Of course, not all neo-Marxist educators have interpreted Marxism to mean that the student was to be liberated from all the conditioning influences of society and tradition; some have argued, for example, that the working class should have access to the more rigorous traditions of a liberal education.[8]

The important point of interest here is not the startling divergent range of educational prescriptions that can be derived from Marxism, but the more basic problem of attempting to develop a theory of education without taking seriously the dynamics of primary socialization. The form of economy does indeed have a relationship with the dominant ideas transmitted in the classroom, but a concern with eliminating economic oppression and social inequality has led the neo-Marxists educators to substitute their vision of an ideal society for a realistic understanding of how socialization occurs. Hegemony, hierarchy, authority, discipline, inequality, and tradition are metaphors that neo-Marxist educators tend to associate with economic exploitation and social injustice. Consequently their proposals for an alternative educational practice tend either toward the Arcadian romanticism expressed by Harris or they represent an uneasy reconciliation of traditional educational values with the language of liberation.

By not taking seriously the transcendent elements of the socialization process, by which I mean the most basic elements that continue to occur in different cultural settings as well as in post-revolutionary societies, the neo-Marxist educators are unable to escape the romantic vision that leads many people either to suspect their true motives or to question their ability to acknowledge that Marxist revolutions have not eliminated exploitive relationships. In effect, socializing the means of production or even redistributing wealth and power on more equitable terms may resolve certain problems but may fail to eliminate the universal problem that is faced by each generation of youth as they acquire the models of thinking that underpin the adult world.

To read the educational prescriptions of the neo-Marxist educational theorists is to enter into an ideally constructed world where the evils denoted by such terms as hegemony, oppression, hierarchy, inequality, tradition, authority, and alienation can be permanently banished by the restructing of society. The image of students freeing themselves from the oppressive forces of history with only the democratic guidance of a radical teacher who allows for the discovery of their free, cooperative, and equalitarian nature suggests a theory that had long ago lost touch with the realities of human nature and the workings of everyday society. Unlike most neo-Marxists educational theorists who avoid discussing the specific educational activities that would be consistant with Marxism, Henry Giroux confronts the problem head on and in the process reveals the difficulty of making the student-teacher relationship fit the ideal framework of the more romantic interpretations of Marxism. On the question of authority Giroux writes that "The democratization and humanization of power in the classroom should not suggest that radical teachers retreat from positions of authority. What is suggested is that we should abandon authority roles that deny the subjectivity and power students have to create and generate their own meanings and visions."[9]

Although it is difficult to reconcile the authority of the teacher with the student's power to "generate their own meanings and vision" it is clear that Giroux is not prepared to abandon entirely the atavistic idea of authority. But how does the teacher justify a claim to authority when it conflicts with expressions of the student's subjectivity? Are there other forms of authority encompassed in Giroux's use of the metaphor? The problem of how to reconcile grades, which he refers to as "soft cops," with the romantic view of the egalitarian and democratic classroom is equally ambiguous. As an alternative to using grades to promote social conformity Giroux suggests that we think of "Dialogical grading . . . an extension of Paulo Freire's emphasis on the role of dialogue among students and teachers over the criteria, function, and consequences of the grading system."[10] Instead of addressing the deeper issue of why the use of grades should be retained, he suggests that the grading process can be democratized by having "students learn how to play a meaningful role in the grading process, one that gives them the opportunity to understand the ideological assumptions behind the choices that determine the process of grading itself."[11] One is inclined to ask how the authority of the grading process would be justified if students, after grasping the teacher's ideological orientation, disagreed with the teacher's right to exercise a judgment about their academic performance. Or will the problem go away by virtue of the fact that the students now possess an understanding of the process?

The awkwardness of Giroux's attempt to reconcile traditional elements of the teacher's authority (he is not talking about authoritarianism) with the neo-Marxist concern with eliminating inequality, class distinctions, and hegemonic forms of culture reflect the problems of developing a theory of education that begins with abstract theory. The writings of the neo-Marxist educators who subscribe to a more humanistic interpretation of Marxism organize the world into strict categories where inequality, hierarchy, class, and hegemony are associated with exploitive capitalism, while self-determination, equality, cooperation, and dialogue are identified with the progressive values of Marxism. Robert Heilbroner has pointed out that Marxists have not examined in any serious way the conservative's caveats about the socialist view of human nature, the redemptive power of the state, and the idea that revolutionaries will always use power in a socially beneficial way.[12] The problem in starting with abstract formulations of how society ought to be organized and then deriving a theory of education from ideal formulations about a free and non-exploitive society, is that the theory fails to take into account the perennial characteristics of the social renewal process as well as the influence that local culture has on providing answers to questions that arise from the human condition.

For our purposes, it is important to identify processes and relationships connected with the process of social renewal that will occur in both pre- and post-revolutionary societies. First, the cultural maps that influence how space and time are organized, as well as regulate both personal and social activities, will be part of the tacit learning communicated as significant others interact with the culturally-uninitiated. The cultural aspect of this form of teaching and learning will generally not be part of a deliberate, consciously-planned activity, but will be a more concomitant aspect of language usage, modelling, and of social messages tacitly shared through interacting in everyday situations. Secondly, much of the communication will be characterized by a natural attitude toward the taken-for-granted nature of the cultural maps. Thirdly, the language that the significant other makes available to the person undergoing socialization in the process of defining "what is" will influence the subsequent pattern of thought until it is made explicit and rethought; even then it may continue to exert an influence. Fourthly, much of the conversation will involve the objectification of what is being communicated, there will even be elements of the cultural maps that will involve reifications. These processes represent the background communication that sustains the social-cultural world, they are also part of the more deliberate part of the socialization process that we call education. A discussion of this social renewal and maintenance process is conspicuously absent from the writings of most neo-Marxist educational theorists.

The categorical thinking which characterizes the neo-Marxist educators' approach fails to take into account how the authority of tradition is reproduced through the different language systems that are used to sustain our everyday world, nor do they recognize that the relationship between the person who shares taken-for-granted knowledge with the uninitiated individual always involves an unequal relationship that involves differences in linguistic competence, as well as the existential confidence that comes with experience. Finally, the neo-Marxists' lack of recognition of the pervasiveness and shaping power of cultural forms of learning brings into question their claims about students liberating themselves from the oppressive traditions of society. In a sense, the failure of the neo-Marxist educators to develop a theory of learning that takes account of what cultural linguistics and the sociology of knowledge (the Schutz-Berger-Luckmann stream) tell us about the relation between culture, language, and thought leads them to making promises that have no theoretical or empirical foundations. Radical politics can indeed lead to fundamental changes in the form of economy and the place where political power is vested in society; while some of the cultural content of what is communicated may be changed most of the pre-revolutionary cultural maps will be retained, as can be seen by documenting the cultural continuities that transcend revolutions. In effect, the dynamics of socialization process continues on regardless of ideological orientation. Understanding the dynamics of socialization does not mean returning to a view of education that isolates what happens in the classroom from the outside economic-political-cultural forces, but it does involve the recognition that the liberation of the mind is always a partial achievement and that today's liberated thought may become tomorrow's reification. It also leads to a genuinely radical approach to learning, but it is radical in the sense of examining the historical and cultural foundations of thought rather than in the sense of using the rhetoric of individuals who see themselves as radical, but who may, in fact, be controlled by the unexamined assumptions of their culture.

THE DIFFICULTY OF THE SOCIOLOGY OF KNOWLEDGE APPROACH

Unlike the neo-Marxist educational theorists who passed over the theory of the social construction of reality in order to engage in a supposedly more politically-oriented theory of schooling, the third group of critics are likely to base their objections on existential grounds that are more difficult with which to deal. The response of some education students who have encountered the Schutz, Berger, and Luckmann framework is that the vocabulary is too unfamiliar and the concepts are more difficult to grasp than those they are accustomed to using. Colleagues who have used *Cultural Literacy for Freedom* also report that many students encounter difficulty when they are invited to think about education within the dialectical framework of the sociology of knowledge. Objections about the centralness of the theory to understanding the educational process do not seem to be raised. The existential problem of being comfortable with other theoretical frameworks that undergird taken-for-granted beliefs, such as behaviorism, is exceedingly difficult one with which to deal. If the vocabulary of the theory framework corresponds to the education student's natural attitude, it will likely leave the student with the same pattern of thinking that would be acquired in other education courses based on a positivist paradigm that incorporates both a subject-object and a fact-value distinction. In effect, to understand the interaction process involving the cultural maps that the participants bring to the moment of socialization (education), as well as the multiple influences of language on the process, it is necessary to introduce a new vocabulary that is not a carrier of the images that organize our conception of reality in the old dichotomous way. The inertia of existential indifference that characterizes some educational students is a phenomena that I am still puzzled about and do not, consequently, have an adequate response for at this time. For the educational students who are put off by a new and seemingly mystifying vocabulary, it would seem that the most appropriate response would be to view the problem in terms of the sociology of knowledge framework that was laid out earlier. Instead of retreating back into theoretical frameworks with which the student is already familiar; the teacher should recognize the conceptual maps that the students bring to their encounter with the vocabulary and theory framework of the sociology of knowledge. The students are encountering what the theory attempts to explain, namely the "moves" in the very complex language game of reality sharing (which can also turn out to be a matter of "reality rejection"). The concepts relating to the political nature of language, how communication of a natural attitude may serve as a model, how objectification occurs, and how the deep patterns (or paradigm) for organizing thought are transmitted through language, must be taught in a systematic manner and, at the same time, be related to the student's phenomenological world. In effect, students majoring in education must be able to understand the theory's explanatory power in terms of their own experience of being socialized; this will help them to ground the theory in a manner that illuminates the culture-language-consciousness dynamic of the classroom.

When students begin to see that the theory provides the vocabulary for naming and thinking about the reality-constituting process that they are undergoing in the classroom, as well as how their sense of reality has been influenced by socialization outside the classroom, the sense of holding the theory at arm's length generally disappears. But as Berger and Luckmann suggest, our sense of social reality is precarious in the sense that communication helps to sustain what we experience as real. For example, if we do not communicate with friends over a long period of time the sense of friendship may become precarious in the sense that we begin to think of them as former friends, or perhaps as acquaintances. Similarly, if education students become familiar with the dialectical thought of the sociology of knowledge, they may begin to think about educational issues within this framework; but if they move into another language environment that involves a different master pattern for organizing thought it may be difficult to maintain the dialectical pattern of thinking. If the education student is subsequently hired as a teacher in a system where communication involves a view of education as measurable, hierarchically organized in a manner that establishes the pre-eminent role of expert knowledge, and involves the teacher as a manager of a learning process that is highly predetermined, it will be difficult to maintain the set educational priorities that characterize thinking within the sociology of knowledge framework. It is not that teachers are plastic in the sense that their environment shapes them; it is more a matter of not being sufficiently grounded in the reality construct of a language framework to recognize that reinforcement is necessary to sustain that sense of reality. As one begins to use the vocabulary of a conflicting paradigm (e.g., learning outcomes, behavioral objectives, competencies, knowledge production), one begins to slip into the paradigm's reality framework. The precariousness of patterns of thinking that are outside the orthodox reality set of mainstream educational thought and practice raises several policy issues that need to be recognized by teacher-training institutions. (I will return later to these policy issues.)

The argument that the theory is too difficult for education students to understand may be followed by the argument that it is too difficult to apply in the classroom. The latter argument, though raised by teachers who may not see the irony of viewing this criticism against the background trend of attempting to make the classroom fit a systems model of thinking, misses an essential point. Although teachers may lack a conceptual framework for recognizing the dynamics of the reality-constituting and maintenance process of socialization, they are nevertheless fully involved. It is not an either-or situation, in which the teacher's professed ignorance or hostility toward thinking within a new framework allows them to be uninvolved. Regardless of the teacher's area of specialization, the medium used is language and the content of what is taught (which cannot really be separated from the medium) represents a part of the culture the student is expected to internalize. Once one recognizes that the sociology of knowledge brings into focus some of the processes that occur as teacher and students interact, it then becomes a matter of approaching the practical implications of the theory framework in a more incremental way.

As suggested previously (Chapter 3), the teacher can use the theory as a way of making explicit what otherwise might be part of the unintended teaching. This would include recognizing the nature of the deeper categories and patterns of thought that enable the student to organize new information and concepts into a coherent view of reality that is shared by other members of the same language community, as well as developing a greater sensitivity concerning taken-for-granted beliefs and reifications. It should also lead to an expanded understanding of learning as a cultural phenomena rather than simply as a process initiated by the teacher.[13] This

. deeper understanding of learning will help the teacher see the student in terms of their ability to learn in cultural contexts where little of the teaching and learning process are made explicit or made to fit the model of classroom learning, but where failure to demonstrate a cultural form of intelligence carries very real consequences. The recognition that the student is a carrier of cultural knowledge that is highly complex, and yet is largely held at the unconscious level, is essential for establishing the connection between the new element of culture (or way of understanding) the teacher wishes to introduce and the cultural maps that the student has already internalized.

A more progressive step in terms of utilizing the sociology of knowledge in the classroom involves being able to use existing curricula in a way that enables the student to make explicit taken-for-granted beliefs and categories of thought. There is then a greater potential that classroom learning can be more frequently moved to the level where the structure of thought itself is examined as both a cultural and historical phenomena. This is already being done by teachers who explore their subject area in terms of the underlying cultural conventions of thought. The sociology of knowledge simply adds to the teacher's understanding of how to avoid communicating their subject as though it existed independently of the historical and cultural forces that produced it. The sociology of knowledge approach also adds to the teacher's understanding of how to utilize the community as a curriculum resource where students can relate the abstract representations of culture (e.g., how we talk and read about work) with how it is "lived" in the community.

Students who collect the folklore by talking to members of the community acquire a greater facility in thinking and talking about this area of their culture than students who only read about the folklore. The same holds true for how students learn about other areas of the curriculum. It is when the teacher is able to integrate a variety of sources into the curriculum—the traditional organization of knowledge in textbooks (often an objectified and consensus view), the cultural knowledge that has been internalized as part of the students' natural attitude, and the more scholarly form of knowledge that enables the teacher to put topics, "facts," and issues into a historical perspective and enables the teacher to pose questions and suggest relationships that expand the student's thought—that the teacher is operating fully within a sociology of knowledge framework. At this point the framework itself becomes a part of the teacher's natural attitude.

COMMUNITIES AND CRITICAL THINKING

This brings us to a fourth area of criticism. That is, the community will not tolerate an approach to education that fosters a critical examination of cultural beliefs and practices. This criticism is often made by school officials and teachers who generalize specific instances of intolerance by community groups into a policy position they can use to justify not doing anything in the classroom that would involve risk. Fortunately, we do not canvas the community on what can be taught in the classroom, though a case could be made that the politics of local control influences what happens in the classroom by virtue of the controls exerted over the selection of administrators and teachers. If we were to canvas the community we would find, in most instances, that the community can only agree on the most abstract generalizations and that issues relating to content and interpretation would reveal deep and often irreconcilable divisions. In most instances, the community is not a unified entity that shares a common set of beliefs, it is more characterized by the syncretism of different reality sets that lead individuals to give accent to commonly shared beliefs only when they do not challenge directly a more personally held set of beliefs. Recognizing the cultural pluralism that underlies the veneer of community cohesiveness points up the difficulty in the argument that the school should teach only what the community wants.

Unless we eliminate the use of the media and severely restrict contact between different groups, it is impossible to limit the socialization that goes on in schools to what the student is exposed to in the home. Clearly this cannot be done, nor will the voucher system insure a symmetry between what is taught in school and in the home. The increased mobility and communication means that the student's horizon will be expanded beyond that of the parents. To argue that local control ("accountability" in today's parlance) means the teacher should not broaden the socialization process beyond what is taught in the home ignores the cultural composition of the community, the influence of a technological society, and the impossibility of achieving any meaningful level of consensus on either the content or treatment of the curriculum. Clearly the community cannot be used as a justification for placing constraints on students' critical understanding of a culture that will be encountered at a less reflective level outside the classroom.

Although the pluralistic nature of most American communities might prevent consensus except at the most ritualistic level of abstraction the teacher must recognize certain responsibilities to the community, even though these responsibilities may never be articulated. These responsibilities relate directly to the teacher's understanding of the sociology of knowledge explanation of the educational process. Understanding the role of communication and the student in the construction of what is experienced as "reality" provides a great deal of power, and this power should be guided by a sense of responsibility to the student as well as, in a more general sense, to the community. Exposing students to explanatory frameworks for understanding different aspects of the life world, as well as making explicit taken-for-granted beliefs and reifications, provides the linguistic and conceptual basis for communicative competence. It is using the dynamics of the socialization process to empower the student, but not in the sense of contributing to an autonomous individual who cannot conceptualize the issues beyond what is dictated by an infantile form of ego-centeredness. The responsibility to the community is expressed in the teacher's sense of fairness in presenting different interpretive frameworks and pertinent evidence and in mediating between divergent expressions of opinion. It also involves a concern with adjusting the socialization process, particularly the influence of social class differences on the distribution of worthwhile knowledge in a manner that contributes to greater equality of opportunity. Finally, teachers have a responsibility to demonstrate a high level of intellectual competence in their subject areas. Though the community may be unable to reach consensus on the issue through the normal political process, the inquiry process is dependent on the teachers knowing their subject area at a depth that enables them to recognize the taken-for-granted beliefs and reifications that would otherwise limit the student's level of understanding. This commitment to maintaining intellectual standards is essential for preventing the inquiry process from being a thinly veiled excuse for substituting the teacher's set of taken-for-granted beliefs for those taught in the home.

This brings me back to the basic point that teachers exercises significant control as to how culture is transmitted in the classroom. Their basic responsibility is to conduct this process in a way that opens the students' minds to the intellectual traditions that have influenced the development of their culture. This responsibility cannot be given over to the community. Recent talk about greater accountability to the community has encouraged dissident community groups to impose their sectarian views in a manner that has limited freedom of inquiry, has led to banning books, and has promoted the rise of the technicist mentality in education as a misguided way of de-politizing the potential area of conflict over education. How the different groups that make up the public think about education is also a social construction that has been influenced by past socialization (how adults learned as students the set of taken-for-granted beliefs that underpin their present views) and by how educators themselves have defined the nature of education. It was the professional educator, and not the public, that defined the teacher's responsibility in terms of the politically-loaded metaphor of "accountability." That the public began to think of the educational process in terms of the language made available to them should not be surprising, given what we understand about the influence of language (in particular, the metaphorical aspect of language) on how we think. The conventional way of thinking about education and the responsibilities of the teacher have changed over time and is amenable to further change as educators introduce new metaphorical language that brings into focus aspects of learning that have been ignored in recent years. As educators understand the relation between a form of education that contributes to the students' communicative competence in the political process of re-negotiating basic aspects of our collective belief system and the cultural values of fairness, equality of opportunities, and respect for intellectual achievement, they will increasingly influence the language that establishes the boundaries within which we think about education. Hopefully, educators will begin to challenge the conventional belief that the public will not tolerate schools that encourage a thoughtful examination of cultural practice, rather than using the folk mythology of local control as an excuse for avoiding the responsibilities that are grounded in a deeper set of cultural values.

A key link in establishing the connection between the educational theory derived from the analysis of the relativizing forces in culture and the sociology of knowledge and what happens in the classroom, is the education of the teacher. As stated earlier, the teacher's power and craft are expressed in a complex language environment that involves the constituting of meanings by students, in terms of their conceptual frameworks, as well as meanings that are dictated by the language systems in use. A typical classroom may involve the use of a number of language systems in a single day, the language of mathematics, science, and social sciences, the more metaphorical language of art, the body language of both students and teacher, and the language systems that regulate the use of social and physical space. What the teacher teaches and for which he or she tests, represents only a minor part of the education that occurs as students learn at both the tacit and explicit levels, often in ways that reflect the interpretative frameworks built up through their own biographies of socialization. Moreover, the language environment of the classroom is highly metaphorical, since the teacher and curriculum take students into cultural territory where the new is often expressed in terms of images taken from other areas of experience with which the student has some acquaintance. Learning to think of something as though it were like something else, as well as internalizing the deep patterns of thought that are reproduced through the metaphorical image, makes learning problematic in ways not often recognized by the teacher or students.

When we begin to view learning in the classroom in a way that brings into focus the synergistic relationship between language and culture, it becomes evident that the education of teachers has been based on fundamentally-incorrect assumptions. The dominant direction of teacher education has been based on the wrong metaphors, with the result that newly trained (as distinct from educated) teachers are even less likely to understand the language systems that they use, nor are they likely to understand how language uses them. The essential problem can be traced to thinking of teaching and learning as though it were like a manufacturing process where the student's behavior was to be shaped by a highly rationalized control of learning inputs. The growing influence of behaviorism, along with the development of techniques borrowed from the ideology of Taylorism, has led to an increasing separation of teaching technique from content area (particularly at the elementary level) and to the rise of educational experts whose self-appointed task has been to produce a plethora of learning systems and packages that would ensure the efficient management of the classroom.

In lamenting the extraordinary imbalance in teacher education programs, I do not want to suggest that all the efforts to make teaching systematic and predictable should be discarded. There is a place for systematic teaching techniques. The problem lies more in the realm of identifying a particular educational problem (learning of basic skills, which is a very real problem) and then generalizing the response to that problem in a way that dominates the entire approach to teacher education. The attempt to ensure that new teachers could demonstrate prescribed levels of competency in teaching specific skills and behaviors exacerbated the tendency to emphasize the learning of techniques at the expense of becoming an educated person. The challenge now is to reform teacher education in a manner that subordinates the technical element to other requirements essential to good teaching. This will involve dropping the practice of thinking of education in terms of the root metaphor of a mechanical universe.

A new metaphorical image for thinking about education and the preparation of teachers might appropriately be borrowed from the anthropological understanding of man as a creator and use of languages. This would create a more generic image for understanding the linguistic foundations of culture and, at the more pedagogical level, the role of the teacher as a transmitter of culture. The technicist image of the teacher distorts our understanding of technology as an expression of a specific cultural pattern of thought. As attention becomes excessively focused on technical procedures, the cultural forces that have shaped both our form of technique and the purposes to which we put it to use are obscured.

This image of what is at the center of educational activity should lead to teacher-education programs placing greater emphasis on the constructionist aspects of cognitive psychology, cultural anthropology, social and cultural linguistics, and the sociology of knowledge. Work in these areas seem fundamental to understanding the nature of learning and to the development of sound pedagogical practices. The use of behaviorism as a theory of learning, on the other hand, leads to the development of techniques that give the teacher a short term strategic advantage in controlling "educational outcomes" (their term), but does not deal with the education of the future teacher. The education of a teacher is a much more complicated issue that requires a broader and more reflexive epistemological framework. As pedagogical theory and practice, as well as curriculum development, are grounded more in the disciplines that focus on the interaction of culture and cognition, the teacher will possess a better grasp of the problem of how theory relates to classroom practice. Too often, education students take one or two courses that provide an introduction to the cultural and cognitive aspects of education and then find themselves taking a great many more strategy-type courses based on the positivist-behaviorist set of assumptions. If we look at the conceptual framework to which teachers are socialized, it is not surprising to see the reason they are unable to understand how either the content of the curriculum or their style of pedagogy is part of the more complex language environment of the classroom. Their own socialization should involve a more in-depth encounter with the cultural and developmental aspects of learning, the symbolic interactionist nature of socialization, and some exposure to thinking about the politics and cultural epistemology of knowledge, followed by courses that help them relate this theory to teaching in the classroom. Assisting prospective teachers to translate this theoretical framework into classroom practice is part of the socialization process that is disrupted by having them take methodology and learning-assessment courses that are based on a different paradigm. They may remember that the courses dealing with the anthropology of learning or Piaget's theory of cognitive development were intellectually interesting, but they remain unable to see how the courses relate to the classroom. The methodology and assessment courses, on the other hand, are initially seen as more "practical" than intellectually interesting; but after the teacher begins to operate in the classroom for awhile the content of these courses begins to slip away because the courses lacks the explanatory power necessary for helping the teacher understand and deal with the symbolic world of the classroom. This is not to say that methodology courses based on positivist-behaviorist assumption are completely devoid of useful information; it is more a matter of putting the insights and practical information that can be gained from this framework in a more subordinate role in the education of teachers.

Not only would a new metaphorical image lead to changes in our approach to the professional part of teacher education, it would also lead to overcoming the schism that too often exists between departments of education and the rest of the university community. The isolation of teacher education involves a complex history of suspicion and misunderstanding on both sides, but a basic consequence of this isolation is that the training rather than the education of the teacher has been emphasized. Except in secondary education, where academic departments exert significant influence on certification requirements, teachers have been certified without any genuine assessment of whether they have acquired a solid academic grounding in the areas they may be asked to teach, or possess a respect for the intellectual processes essential to making education into a liberalizing experience. In the earlier discussion of the teacher's responsibility to the community, it was suggested that any claim to freedom of inquiry in the classroom involved an obligation on the teacher's part to possess a sufficient knowledge of their subject area to be able to present information accurately, to recognize taken-for-granted beliefs and reifications, and to be able to put issues, events, and factual knowledge into some form of a historical and cultural perspective. Without this depth of understanding, teaching becomes largely a matter of socializing students to the limited pattern of thinking contained in the textbooks and curriculum guides. While this process does not require freedom of inquiry, it is not likely to be approved by the more reflective members of the community, nor is it likely to provide students with the mental capacities they will need in any future negotiation of the social understandings and practices that are to govern everyday life.

Another reason for closer cooperation between teacher education departments and the liberal arts faculty has to do with the isolation of the public school teacher from the knowledge explosion occurring in universities. After teachers complete their own formal education and receive certification, they face the problem of possessing knowledge that becomes obsolete as the frontiers of knowledge in their field are advanced. The physical, psychological, and intellectual burdens of teaching, particularly when the school is organized along the lines of a business operation, make it exceedingly difficult to keep intellectually current, much less to have the time to reflect on what constitutes seminal knowledge as opposed to the intellectual fads and false starts. A more cooperative relationship between the faculties of teacher education and liberal arts would make it easier for teacher education departments to provide workshops, seminars, and retreats that would provide classroom teachers with the opportunity to learn about new areas of knowledge and to discuss how this knowledge could be introduced into the classroom. In effect, the teacher-education faculty could serve as a bridge between the scholars and the classroom teacher. Instead of requiring teachers to return to the campus for the purpose of taking professional courses that deal with technique, the teachers could participate in a seminar or workshop that provides exposure to new work being done in their field of interest. Courses dealing with classroom management and teaching techniques, which are often taken for purposes more directly related to salary advancement than intellectual curiosity, cannot compensate for the teacher's inability to exercise an informed judgment about how major new developments in their primary area of academic interest can be introduced into the curriculum. The knowledge explosion makes the task of keeping intellectually-current a nearly impossible task for the full time academic. The concern here is not in adding to the excessive burdens that public schoolteachers already experience; rather it is to get the priorities straight on what helps the classroom teachers provide a more adequate education for students and to emphasize those activities that assist teachers in this task.

As we discuss the more practical aspects of the dominant ideological orientation in teacher education the impossibility of separating technical considerations from questions pertaining to content and the dynamics of cultural transmission becomes more evident. Ultimately, one must ask the question whether the socialization process in the classroom contributes to the student's ability to understand the conceptual foundations of the major problems confronting society. Communicative competence, in the full sense of that phrase, thus becomes the litmus test of the adequacy of the theories that guide our approach to the education of teachers.

NOTES

1. Manfred Stanley, "On Throwing Out Babies and Other Metaphors: A Comment on Bowers' Review of the *Technological Conscience*," *Teachers College Record 82* (Summer 1981): 675–687. Also see Donald L. Carveth, "The Disembodies Dialectic: A Psychoanalytic Critic of Sociological Relativisim," *Theory and Society 4* (Spring 1977); and Michael F. D. Young, "Taking Sides against the Probable Problems of Relativism and Commitment in Teaching and the Sociology of Knowledge," *Educational Review 25* (1973).
2. For a discussion of the elements of modern thought that contribute to nihilism see Johan Goudsblom, *Nihilism and Culture* (Totowa, N.J.: Rowman ano Littlefield, 1980); Stanley Rosen, *Nihilism: A Philosophic Essay* (New Haven: Yale University Press, 1969); and Charles Glicksberg, *The Literature of Nihilism* (Lewisburg, Pa.: Bucknell University Press, 1975).
3. Geoff Whitty, "Sociology and the Problem of Radical Educational Change," in *Educability, Schools and Ideology*, ed. Michael Flude and John Ahier (London: Halstead, 1974), 125.
4. Kevin Harris, *Education and Knowledge* (London: Routledge and Kegan Paul, 1979), 179.
5. Ibid., 188.
6. Samual Bowles and Herbert Gintis, *Schooling in Capitalist America* (New York: Basic Books, 1976), 273.
7. Henry A. Giroux, *Idealogy, Culture and the Process of Schooling* (Philadelphia: Temple University Press, 1981), 85.
8. David Reynolds and Michael Sullivan, "Towards a New Socialist Sociology of Education," in *Schooling, Ideology and the Curriculum*, ed. Len Barton, Roland Meighan, and Stephen Walker (Barcombe, Lewes: Falmer Press, 1980).
9. Giroux, *Process of Schooling*, 84.
10. Ibid.
11. Ibid.
12. Robert L. Heilbronner, "A Radical View of Socialism," *Social Research 39* (Spring 1972): 1–15.
13. An excellent introduction to the process by which individuals "acquire" a knowledge of their culture, including its options and commands, can be found in Harry F. Wolcott, "The Anthropology of Learning," *Anthropology and Educational Quarterly 13* (Summer 1982): 83–107.

Index